AN ADULT EVENING OF SHEL SILVERSTEIN

BY SHEL SILVERSTEIN

DRAMATISTS
PLAY SERVICE
INC.

AN ADULT EVENING WITH SHEL SILVERSTEIN
Copyright © 2003, Estate of Shel Silverstein

All Rights Reserved

CAUTION: Professionals and amateurs are hereby warned that performance of any or all of the Plays in the volume AN ADULT EVENING WITH SHEL SILVERSTEIN is subject to payment of a royalty. The Plays are fully protected under the copyright laws of the United States of America, and of all countries covered by the International Copyright Union (including the Dominion of Canada and the rest of the British Commonwealth), and of all countries covered by the Pan-American Copyright Convention, the Universal Copyright Convention, the Berne Convention, and of all countries with which the United States has reciprocal copyright relations. All rights, including without limitation professional/amateur stage rights, motion picture, recitation, lecturing, public reading, radio broadcasting, television, video or sound recording, all other forms of mechanical, electronic and digital reproduction, transmission and distribution, such as CD, DVD, the Internet, private and file-sharing networks, information storage and retrieval systems, photocopying, and the rights of translation into foreign languages are strictly reserved. Particular emphasis is placed upon the matter of readings, permission for which must be secured from the Author's agent in writing.

The English language stock and amateur stage performance rights in the United States, its territories, possessions and Canada for the Plays in the volume AN ADULT EVENING WITH SHEL SILVERSTEIN are controlled exclusively by DRAMATISTS PLAY SERVICE, INC., 440 Park Avenue South, New York, NY 10016. No professional or nonprofessional performance of any or all of the Plays may be given without obtaining in advance the written permission of DRAMATISTS PLAY SERVICE, INC., and paying the requisite fee.

Inquiries concerning all other rights should be addressed to Rosenstone Adams, 448 West 44th Street, New York, NY 10036 or rosenstone@bretadamsltd.com.

SPECIAL NOTE

Anyone receiving permission to produce any or all of the Plays in the volume AN ADULT EVENING WITH SHEL SILVERSTEIN is required to give credit to the Author as sole and exclusive Author of the Play(s) on the title page of all programs distributed in connection with performances of the Play(s) and in all instances in which the title(s) of the Play(s) appears for purposes of advertising, publicizing or otherwise exploiting the Play(s) and/or a production thereof. The name of the Author must appear on a separate line, in which no other name appears, immediately beneath the title(s) and in size of type equal to 50% of the size of the largest, most prominent letter used for the title(s) of the Play(s). No person, firm or entity may receive credit larger or more prominent than that accorded the Author. The following acknowledgment must appear on the title page in all programs distributed in connection with performances of the Play(s):

Originally Produced in New York City
by Atlantic Theater Company, 2001–02.

AN ADULT EVENING OF SHEL SILVERSTEIN was produced by the Atlantic Theater Company (Neil Pepe, Artistic Director; Beth Emelson, Producing Director) in New York City on September 9, 2001. It was directed by Karen Kohlhaas; the set design was by Walt Spangler; the lighting design was by Robert Perry; the costume design was by Miguel Angel Huidor; the sound design was by Malcolm Nicholls; the general manager was Ryan Freeman; the production manager was Kurt Gardner; and the production stage manager was Christa Bean. The cast was as follows:

ONE TENNIS SHOE
Harvey .... Jordan Lage
Sylvia .... Maryann Urbano
BUS STOP
Irwin .... Josh Stamberg
Celia .... Alicia Goranson
GOING ONCE
Auctioneer .... Jody Lambert
Annie .... Kelly Maurer
THE BEST DADDY
Lisa .... Alicia Goranson
Daddy .... Jordan Lage
THE LIFEBOAT IS SINKING
Jen .... Kelly Maurer
Sherwin .... Josh Stamberg
SMILE
Bender .... Kelly Maurer
Gibby .... Jody Lambert
Jimbo .... Jordan Lage
Snooky .... Josh Stamberg
WASH AND DRY
Marianne .... Alicia Goranson
Georgia .... Maryann Urbano
THINKING UP A NEW NAME FOR THE ACT
Lucy .... Kelly Maurer
Pete .... Jody Lambert
BUY ONE, GET ONE FREE
Merilee .... Alicia Goranson
Sherilee .... Maryann Urbano
Lee .... Jordan Lage
BLIND WILLIE AND THE TALKING DOG
Blind Willie .... Josh Stamberg
Barney .... Jordan Lage

CONTENTS

ONE TENNIS SHOE 5
BUS STOP 12
GOING ONCE 14
THE BEST DADDY 17
THE LIFEBOAT IS SINKING 21
SMILE 27
WASH AND DRY 31
THINKING UP A NEW NAME FOR THE ACT 40
BUY ONE, GET ONE FREE 45
BLIND WILLIE AND THE TALKING DOG 51

AN ADULT EVENING OF SHEL SILVERSTEIN

ONE TENNIS SHOE

HARVEY. This is not going to be easy to say.
SYLVIA. Try.
HARVEY. It's not an easy subject to discuss —
SYLVIA. What is it?
HARVEY. Well okay — okay.
WAITER. Can I get you anything else?
HARVEY. No. No thank you.
WAITER. Very good.
SYLVIA. What? What? Are you sick? Are you — ?
HARVEY. I'm fine —
SYLVIA. You're having an affair — you're in love with somebody else —
HARVEY. No, I'm fine — I love you —
SYLVIA. Well, then what?
HARVEY. I can't — say it —
SYLVIA. Then don't say it — I want another espresso —
HARVEY. I've got to say it — I'm going to say it — you — are — becoming — a —
SYLVIA. Yes — yes — what — ? I'm becoming a what? I'm becoming a nag? I'm becoming a bore? What?
HARVEY. Worse.
SYLVIA. Nothing is worse than a bore. Harvey — what? What am I becoming?
HARVEY. You — are becoming a — you are turning into a — a — bag lady.

SYLVIA. A bag lady —
HARVEY. Yes. That's the hardest thing I'll ever have to say.
SYLVIA. I'm turning into a bag lady.
HARVEY. Yes, I'm afraid you are.
SYLVIA. I assume you mean one of those crazy old raggy ladies who pick things out of garbage cans and carry all their clothes in shopping bags and have lice in their hair and talk to themselves — I assume we're talking about the same ladies.
HARVEY. I didn't say you had lice in your hair.
SYLVIA. But you did say I was a bag lady.
HARVEY. I said turning *into* — not *was* —
SYLVIA. Turning into a bag lady — well, that's pretty much like turning into a werewolf, isn't it?
HARVEY. Please — I'm just trying to —
SYLVIA. You are trying to tell me I'm a bag lady.
HARVEY. It's been evident for some time — you've been showing signs for quite some time.
SYLVIA. Signs —
HARVEY. Indications — symptoms — manifestations —
SYLVIA. Of becoming a bag lady.
HARVEY. Yes.
SYLVIA. There's no chance that you could be mistaken — you're sure.
HARVEY. I wish I *was* mistaken — I want to be wrong.
SYLVIA. Well, I think I'd like a second opinion.
HARVEY. I'm serious about this.
SYLVIA. Harvey — look at me. Tell me — look at me, Harvey — wouldn't you say I was a little too young to be a bag lady? Maybe a little too old to be queen of the prom — but just a teensy weensy too young to be an old bag lady?
HARVEY. You think old bag ladies started out as old bag ladies? They started out as young women and then —
SYLVIA. And then they went to a wild party and somebody slipped them a shopping bag and it was all over.
HARVEY. I'm trying to make you understand —
SYLVIA. That I am a bag lady — because I am carrying a singular shopping bag — a Bloomingdale's shopping bag — that makes me — a bag lady — oh — Harvey — you are such a schmuck.

HARVEY. It's not because of carrying a shopping bag — it is because of what's *in* the bag —
SYLVIA. Because of what's in the bag?
HARVEY. Yes.
SYLVIA. Well I'm sorry if the contents of my bag don't meet your standards — from now on I'll try to carry only Gucci shoes and Pierre Cardin —
HARVEY. I'm not talking about —
SYLVIA. You're telling me what to carry in my bag.
HARVEY. I'm telling you what *not* to carry.
SYLVIA. What not to carry — what should I not carry, Harvey? What should I not carry so that you will not think I am a bag lady? Tell me and I'll stop carrying it — tell me — tell me —
HARVEY. A sweater.
SYLVIA. A sweater.
HARVEY. And a plastic raincoat.
SYLVIA. A sweater and a raincoat make me a bag lady.
HARVEY. And a tennis shoe.
SYLVIA. Raincoat, sweater and tennis shoes make me a —
HARVEY. Tennis *shoe* — *shoe* singular — one shoe.
SYLVIA. One shoe makes me a bag lady.
HARVEY. Why are you carrying one tennis shoe?
SYLVIA. I'm taking it down to the Bowery — to meet my wino lover — my one-legged wino lover — on Avenue B.
HARVEY. May I inquire about the picture frame?
SYLVIA. What about it?
HARVEY. A picture frame — you tell me about it.
SYLVIA. It's a picture frame — beveled wood — probably pine — approximately nine by twelve with a wire —
HARVEY. *Why* the picture frame?
SYLVIA. Why indeed — how about to hang a picture with? How about that?
HARVEY. *Why* did you pick it up — out of the garbage can? That's what I —
SYLVIA. Not out of the garbage — it was *next* to the can — leaning against the can — not touching the garbage.
HARVEY. Why did you pick it up from next to the can?
SYLVIA. Well, how can I hang a picture in it if I didn't pick it up?

HARVEY. Why didn't you buy a frame?
SYLVIA. Why buy a frame when this is a perfectly good frame?
HARVEY. That somebody threw away.
SYLVIA. Yes, that somebody threw away —
HARVEY. And the couch cushion —
SYLVIA. It's a perfectly good cushion — I can use it on my desk chair.
HARVEY. So you just took it.
SYLVIA. When this cushion is covered in a blue floral pattern it will be so —
HARVEY. And the magazines — all the magazines —
SYLVIA. Why are you attacking me like this? What's *really* bothering you?
HARVEY. This — this is what's really bothering me — what could bother a man more than seeing his wife collecting picture frames and tennis shoes and —
SYLVIA. Well, don't forget the grapes while you're at it.
HARVEY. You have grapes in there?
SYLVIA. I have everything in here — I'm a bag lady, aren't I?
HARVEY. You *are* a bag lady — you say you have grapes and tennis shoes in there like it's perfectly normal — it is not normal — you *are* a bag lady.
SYLVIA. A moment ago I was *becoming* a bag lady — now I *am* a bag lady.
HARVEY. A moment ago I didn't know about the grapes.
SYLVIA. The grapes make me a bag lady.
HARVEY. The grapes *and* the raincoat and the tennis shoe —
SYLVIA. Stop harping on the tennis shoe — if the tennis shoe offends you I'll get rid of it — There — all right?
HARVEY. And the rest of the stuff.
SYLVIA. You want me to throw it all away? I will — I can just leave the bag here and walk away.
HARVEY. I just want you to —
SYLVIA. Except for the picture frame —
HARVEY. That's what I —
SYLVIA. We can leave the rest right here —
HARVEY. Sylvia, do you not see what is happening to you?
SYLVIA. What is happening to me is you — you're attacking me —

HARVEY. I'm trying to reach you — I'm trying to make you see what you're doing.
SYLVIA. I'm not *doing* anything. I just found a nice little picture frame and you turn it into a —
HARVEY. We can stop this now — if we're aware of it we can nip it in the bud —
SYLVIA. I don't see what needs nipping — what? What am I doing?
HARVEY. Will you do me a favor? One favor.
SYLVIA. What is it?
HARVEY. Open your purse.
SYLVIA. Why?
HARVEY. As a favor to me — as a whim.
SYLVIA. Why should I cater to your whims?
HARVEY. Will you open your purse?
SYLVIA. You think there's another tennis shoe in my purse?
HARVEY. Will you — open your purse? Will you open your purse?
SYLVIA. No.
HARVEY. Will you allow me —
SYLVIA. A woman's bag — purse — is a personal thing —
HARVEY. I'm going to open this purse — *(She releases it.)*
SYLVIA. You will *not* find another tennis shoe.
HARVEY. *(Opens purse — looks away — then looks at her — he extends purse toward her.)* Look — *(She looks away)* Look — *(She darts a glance.)* Please look at this purse — *(She nervously looks.)* What do you see? What? What do you see in your purse? *(Sylvia mumbles.)* What? *(Sylvia mumbles again.)* Speak out — let me hear you —
SYLVIA. *Oatmeal — oatmeal!* All right?
HARVEY. *Oatmeal!*
SYLVIA. Yes — are you happy now? Are you satisfied — you sadistic son-of-a-bitch — *oatmeal —*
HARVEY. *Cooked* oatmeal.
SYLVIA. Yes — cooked oatmeal — cold cooked oatmeal — you are vicious — you knew there was oatmeal in that purse — you know it.
HARVEY. I want *you* to know it. I want you to see it.

SYLVIA. I see it — I see it.
HARVEY. Now — Why? — Why — is your purse filled — filled to the brim with old cold wet cooked oatmeal.
SYLVIA. I *see* it's filled with oatmeal.
HARVEY. *Why?*
SYLVIA. Oh Harvey — I —
HARVEY. *(Gently.)* Why, Sylvia, why?
SYLVIA. I don't know.
HARVEY. Do you want a purse full of oatmeal?
SYLVIA. No —
HARVEY. Does *any* woman want a purse full of cooked oatmeal? Do anybody need that?
SYLVIA. No —
HARVEY. Do *you* need it?
SYLVIA. No — I don't think so.
HARVEY. You don't *think* so?
SYLVIA. No — I *know* — I don't need it.
HARVEY. Then why is it there, Sylvia?
SYLVIA. I — don't know.
HARVEY. It's there because you put it there.
SYLVIA. I'm so embarrassed.
HARVEY. All right — so *you* put it there — didn't you.
SYLVIA. I suppose so — yes.
HARVEY. And you got it where?
SYLVIA. Please, you've made your point — I can't —
HARVEY. Where did you get the oatmeal? Did you cook it this morning at home? Did you cook it and then pour it into your purse?
SYLVIA. No.
HARVEY. Did you *buy* it?
SYLVIA. Buy it?
HARVEY. Then you found it — somewhere.
SYLVIA. Stouffers.
HARVEY. Stouffers — You went into Stouffers for breakfast and you —
SYLVIA. For coffee.
HARVEY. And you saw a bowl of oatmeal on the next table and reached —

SYLVIA. On the same table — *(Pause.)* on the table where I sat down. They hadn't cleared the table yet.
HARVEY. You sat down at a dirty table.
SYLVIA. It was crowded — they were busy.
HARVEY. And you emptied it out of the bowl into your purse.
SYLVIA. I didn't empty it — I put it in my purse — all of it.
HARVEY. The *bowl* too — *(He pokes two fingers into purse and half pulls out oatmeal bowl — he pushes it back down and snaps purse shut.)* Sylvia — What does this make you?
SYLVIA. The oatmeal?
HARVEY. The oatmeal and the hubcap and the ketchup bottle and the chicken bones. Chicken bones, Sylvia. You're an intelligent woman — what does this — *(Lifts purse.)* make you?
SYLVIA. A — bag — lady? I don't want to turn into a bag lady, Harvey — I don't want to push a supermarket cart down the street talking to myself and screaming at everybody — I don't want to sleep in a doorway —
HARVEY. You'll never sleep in a doorway —
SYLVIA. This is how it starts — the oatmeal — and shopping bags — then talking to myself, then screaming at people on the street and rummaging through garbage cans and begging for money and not bathing and weaving things into my hair and growing a moustache and drinking wine and sleeping in doorways and getting arrested — oh my God, Harvey, don't let them arrest me — don't let me sleep in the doorway, please, Harvey — please —
HARVEY. Don't get hysterical —
SYLVIA. And if I start weaving that crazy stuff into my hair you've got to stop me — slap me —
HARVEY. I could never slap —
SYLVIA. You've *got* to — you must — Try it — do it now. Slap me.
HARVEY. Sylvia, I can't just slap —
SYLVIA. Slap me and I'll leave this whole bag right where it is — bring me to my senses and we can go home —
HARVEY. Sylvia —
SYLVIA. You've got to be forceful, Harvey. They have no homes — they prowl the streets — they don't get their hair done — they don't have to bathe — they don't have to shave their legs — they

don't worry about it — No cooking to do — no house to clean — No man to — *consider.* They scream out "Hey buster, watch your fender — you son-of-a-bitch — Watch out, you rotten creep — Fuck you, pompous self-righteous — Kiss — me." Ow! *(Slap.)* Thank you, Harvey — I'm leaving that bag right there — We can go home. I'm all right now!
HARVEY. I just wanted you to be aware of —
SYLVIA. I'm grateful — you saved me, I'm lucky to have you, Harvey. I'm going to take this sandwich home for later —
HARVEY. Sylvia …
SYLVIA. That's all right — I don't need it. Wait a minute — what if they see we're leaving the bag — what if the waitress sees — and shouts — "Hey lady, you're forgetting your bag" — I'd die of embarrassment, Harvey, I'll tell you what — I'll take it outside and we can dump it in the nearest trash basket — Now, I know there's a large basket over on Third Avenue and Fifty-Seventh — oh, wait — there's a better one on Fifty-Ninth Street — we can just — *(She continues to talk as they exit and the curtain falls.)*

BUS STOP

Irwin stands on street corner. He is a little drunk and very happy. In one hand he holds a beer can. In the other he holds a pointed "Bus Stop" sign. He sings softly. Celia enters. Irwin steps toward her, holding up sign.

IRWIN. *Bus stop!*
CELIA. What?
IRWIN. Bus stop.
CELIA. I'm not waiting for a bus.
IRWIN. Not *bus* stop — *Bust* stop.
CELIA. Bus…?
IRWIN. *Bust* — B-U-S-T — see the *T?* Tiny T? *Bust* stop. You got the *bust? Stop. (He uses point of sign to point.)* You got the

bazooms? You got the *cans?* The *headlights?* You got the *knockers?* The *Hogans?* The *Hermans?* — *Stop.* You got the *mams,* ma'am? ... *Jugs* — I forgot *jugs* — You got the *jugs?* — *Stop* — in the name of *love* — You got the *melons?* The *pointers?* The — *boobs?* The *boobies?* The *titties?* I hate the word *tits* — I do — *titties*, okay — but tits — it's demeaning. *Cows* have tits — *teats* — there's got to be an *udder* word. Ha ha ha — an *udder* word? — for tits? — You got the ... *(thinks, mouths possibilities — counts on fingers.)* The *mounds* — the *apples* — the *lung warts* — the *Hogans* ... *Jesus* — *Jesus Christ almighty* — *Jesus*, I forgot — *breasts* — *breasts* — the most obvious word and I forget it — How can that be? That we ignore the *obvious* — no pun intended — the thing that ... that pokes us in the *eye* — no pun intended — Why do we overlook — the obvious in search of the — obscure? Is it that the obvious holds no fascination for us — reality holds no charm? Only our own poetry — our own ... *(She advances on him — he backs up.)* Fantastic exaggeration? *Those* draw us, *compel* us.
CELIA. So — ? So what do you *want?*
IRWIN. What?
CELIA. What do you want to *do?*
IRWIN. I want to — find another synonym — jugs, cans, boobs — *hooters* — I forgot *hooters* —
CELIA. I stopped — you said *bust stop* — I got the *bust* — I *stopped* — I got the jugs, the boobies, the globes, the cans, the cleavage, the pillows, the chee-chees, the boobs, the boobies, the bosom, the bazooms, the knockers, the tits, the titties, the *bust* — the bust stops here — *here* — the bristols ... You wanna *see?* — *(Advances.)* You wanna *touch?* — You wanna *lick?* — *chew?* — *nibble?* You wanna put something between 'em? You wanna put your little dickie between 'em? Your little *pee-pee?* — Your big *prick?* Your little *peter?* Your *pecker?* Your *cock?* Your *eel? (She is battering him into the ground.)* Your *prick?* Your — hot *meat?* Your *schlang?* Your *schvants?* — *(She uses the pointed "Bus Stop" sign to make her "point" — she grabs sign and points with it.)* Your *salami?* Your *banger?* Your *wanker?* Your *joy stick?* Your *ding-a-ling?* Your *dong?* Your *prick?* Your *wing dang doodle?* Your *love muscle?* Your *trouser snake?* Your *red helmet warrior?* Your *purple-veined throbber?* Your *tool?* Your *unit?* Your *shaft?* Your *little Elvis?* Your *meat sucker?* Your

one-eyed monster? Your *third leg?* Your *danglin' doozie?* Your *stiff proposition?* Your *rod?* Your *prod?* Your *poker?* Your *pud?* Your *penie?* Your *weenie?* Your *wanker?* Your *pole?* Your *dick?* Your *dork?* Your *bone?* Your *pork?* Your *sausage?* Your *worm?* Your *dummy?* Your *doggin'?* Your *rope?* Your *hose?* Your *whammer?* Your *slammer?* Your *rammer?* Your *rail?* Your *creamer?* Your *club?* Your *flasher?* Your *basher?* Your *shorty?* Your *softie?* Your *sword?* ... *(She stands over him as he simpers and whimpers, continuing her barrage as the lights fade.)*

GOING ONCE

AUCTIONEER. Okay. Now I'll tell you what — It's an auction — that's right — Now you're gonna say, "Oh that's a shame — that's like slavery — that's like selling off an animal." Well, as far as the slavery part, let me tell you, friends — She wants it — she's askin' for it — Aren't you, Annie? Speak up goddamnit — Tell them I'm no Simon Legree — goddamnit — I've got no hold on this woman — I don't own her for God's sake — I'm acting as an agent so don't go callin' me no son-of-a-bitch. I don't go where you work and cuss you out for selling cornflakes or elevator shoes or Ford Grenadas that fall apart as soon as you drive 'em off the lot so don't call me no slave driver — I ain't drivin' her I'm sellin' her — and I ain't keeping the money — twelve percent standard auction fee — that's what I get — she gets the rest — So let's drop the slave stuff and as for the animal part — does this look like an animal to you — turn around, Annie. Okay — show 'em your teeth. Show 'em. *(He reaches in and pulls her mouth open.)* There you go, only one missing — way in the back — only — two — fillings and one that looks like it could use a filling — I'm not gonna bullshit you — I'm not going to misrepresent and sell you damaged goods — okay — I hear it — I hear it — Just like a horse — He's showing her just like a horse — Well I'll tell you something — A woman's teeth *are* just as important as a horse's and a lot more important — you got a horse — that horse gets a rotten tooth,

that horse is gonna still pull his weight — And he ain't gonna bitch about it — but a woman's got a voice — let 'em hear your voice Annie …
ANNIE. Hello.
AUCTIONEER. Let 'em hear you say — "My tooth hurts."
ANNIE. My tooth hurts.
AUCTIONEER. Louder.
ANNIE. My tooth hurts.
AUCTIONEER. Now lets hear a string of 'em run together.
ANNIE. My tooth hurts my tooth hurts my tooth hurts …
AUCTIONEER. Okay how'd you like to listen to that all day and all night? You'd wish she was a horse — Now you ask, "What will she do — If I do invest this whole lot of money, what do I get for it?" — Well that's a fair question — A *sensible* question — Heck, if you *didn't* ask that question, I'd think something was wrong with you. Okay — what will she do? — *Anything* — that's right — you heard me — A-N-Y-T-H-I-N-G — And *everything* — show 'em your tits Annie — (*She unbuttons blouse.*) — Show 'em — you'll be showin 'em later so you might as well show 'em now — We got nothing to hide — Let 'em see what they're buyin' — (*He pulls open blouse.*) Okay — no foam rubber here — no stuffed bra — No silicone — Now please — Please spare me this feigned indignation — "Oh he's showing her breasts" — Yes I'm showing her breasts — And don't pretend breasts don't matter — they matter *plenty* — let's stop the hypocrisy for God's sake — breasts *matter* — And I don't mean just for nursing babies — I'm not promising you three generations — Am I? But say you got her washing the car — or trimming the hedges, well how bad is it to walk up and grab a little feel — you tell me how bad it is. A lot better than those little peanut titties that ain't even a pinch-full let alone a handful — and a lot better than them watermelon juggers — that look good for about two years and then fall to her knees — You tell me — you've seen 'em — And you've seen them fried eggs and flapjacks — and marble in a sock — you seen 'em all now take a look at these — Look but don't touch — And that's all you're gonna see — we're not here to give you a free show are we, Annie? Hell no — we're here to sell a person. Please please — I've heard it all — I've heard it — You're offended — If this was Barbra

Streisand or Olivia Newton-John here or if this was Raquel Welch or Zsa-Zsa Gabor or Sophie's Choice or Rosemary Clooney or any one of them — And I was *their* agent — then it would be okay — then I could sell their voices or their asses or whatever and you'd say fine and dandy — And — And you'd pay twenty dollars plus entertainment tax for the privilege of seeing their show and you wouldn't own *nothing*. Not a damn thing. You'd walk out of there with less than you walked in with. And you might not even have seen a good show — they don't guarantee you a good performance — they guarantee to show up — and some of 'em don't even show up — Judy Garland — case in point — okay — now getting back to what will she do? — She'd do what you want her to do — you pay her price — we'll get to price in a minute — you pay the price and she's yours — Not for the night like some ladies we've seen — not for a year or two until they can get a divorce — like some ladies we *know* — but *forever* — for — ever — So anybody who was thinking they might find a two-dollar bargain — better fold up their tent like the A-RABS and silently steal away — No two-dollar special here — No two-*hundred*-dollar misunderstanding — no two-thousand-*dollar arrangement* — no two-hundred-thousand-dollar — well if you've got two hundred thou then, stick around and we might do some business — right, Annie — show 'em your things — not too much — This ain't no giveaway — let's not let our enthusiasm carry us away eh? Okay what will she do. For those who don't know what *everything* encompasses let me enumerate — she will *(Counts on fingers.)* wash the windows, scrub the floors, do the dishes, do the laundry, type your letters, make the beds, trim your hair, trim your nails, trim the hedges, *(He cops feel.)* weed the flowers, cook soup — cook stews — cook bouillabaisse — bake pies — cakes — cookies and croissants — She'll brew coffee — make biscuits — fry — bake, boil or broil — meats — poultry, fish or veal — She'll answer the phone — answer the doorbell, answer your correspondence — She'll go to church and sing like an angel or stay up and do cocaine all night. She'll drive the car, wash the car, fix the car, simonize the car — She'll sing you songs, read you books, tell you stories. She'll dance — waltz — polka — rumba — samba — go-go-disco — Charleston or Black Bottom — She'll paint the house — strip the furniture — mix martinis, rub your shoulders — She'll play gin rummy, throw darts, bowl in the two hundreds — She'll tell jokes, share smokes, fuck, suck and make the bed and if that ain't everything it'll have to do until everything comes along. If that ain't everything just fill in the blank spaces — I don't have to draw you pictures — do I? Do I? I mean there are minors present — I don't personally give a damn what anybody does behind closed doors and I'm not going to elaborate just to give a few voyeurs some cheap verbal thrills — Okay now — Now — Let's talk turkey — let's get this show going — because *somebody* — some one person — and notice I did not say *man* — I said person — hey there are minors present *(He winks.)* some *one* person and I say *one* so don't think you're going to form some cooperative conglomerate or something like that — this ain't no carpool for God's sake — *one* person — some *one* person is going to walk away with this unique piece of merchandise and the rest of you are going to walk off talking to yourselves and giggling with each other and tomorrow you're gonna wake up with nothing — nothing but a memory that is fading fast — while that one person who is smart enough — enterprising enough — and — and rich enough — oh yes — oh yes — this is not a charity bazaar — rich — rich will scratch the itch — poor will hit the door — money talks and bullshit — well — bullshit doesn't even have the strength to walk — bullshit just lays there — So who is that person — that one person gonna be? Is it gonna be *you?* You tell me. Lemme hear an opening bid of one hundred dollars ... *(Lights fade.)*

THE BEST DADDY

LISA. Okay?
DAD. A little further.
LISA. Here? Can I open my eyes?
DAD. Hold my arm.
LISA. I'm going to bump into it.
DAD. You won't bump into anything. Keep your eyes closed.

Now hold my arm, a couple more steps here.
LISA. Can I look now?
DAD. All right ... Open your eyes right ... now.
LISA. Is that him, there?
DAD. That's right.
LISA. Why is he covered with a blanket?
DAD. Well, he ...
LISA. He doesn't look like a pony.
DAD. Well he is, a thoroughbred gelding 350-dollar Shetland pony.
LISA. Is he laying down?
DAD. Um yes.
LISA. Why is he laying down? Is he sick?
DAD. Pure strain Kentucky-bred Shetland.
LISA. Why is he laying down?
DAD. Lisa ... I didn't want to tell you this ...
LISA. Why is he laying down? He is sick, he is.
DAD. He's dead.
LISA. He ... he's dead?
DAD. It's a helluva thing to have to tell your daughter on her birthday.
LISA. Dead? A dead pony?
DAD. We've got to face the facts.
LISA. You ... you got me a dead pony for my birthday?
DAD. I didn't get you a dead pony for your birth ...
LISA. What happened to him?
DAD. Lisa, I'm going to be honest with you ...
LISA. What happened to my pony?
DAD. You're thirteen years old now and I'm going to talk to you like an adult ...
LISA. What happened to my pony?
DAD. I shot him.
LISA. Y — you shot him?
DAD. About an hour ago, but hear me out.
LISA. Y — you shot my pony? You ... you shot my birthday pony?
DAD. I told you not to get excited, didn't I? Answer me, did I or did I not say, "Don't get too excited ... "

LISA. Why did you shoot my pony?
DAD. I did not shoot your pony. He wasn't your pony when I shot him. You didn't even know he existed. He was a pony.
LISA. Why did you shoot a pony?
DAD. He bit me.
LISA. But you didn't have to shoot him. You didn't have to ... he's only a little pony. He didn't know what he was doing.
DAD. You weren't there, you don't know the situation.
LISA. My pony is dead. I'm thirteen years old today and you gave me a dead pony for my birthday.
DAD. I told you, he bit me.
LISA. But you gave him to me anyway. You took me out here to show me a dead pony?
DAD. Well, I thought about that. I thought, Well, if I take her out here and show her a dead pony that will upset her, but if I don't give her anything she'll think I forgot her birthday.
LISA. What could be worse than getting a dead pony for your birthday?
DAD. Listen now, someday you'll have children of your own. I never shot a pony before. I want you to believe that, never in my life before today.
LISA. You hated my pony, you always hated him.
DAD. I didn't always hate him, I never even ...
LISA. You did. You hated him because you knew I loved him.
DAD. When I saw him I liked him, he was cute.
LISA. You knew he loved me and he could show his feelings and you couldn't stand that. Oh no 'cause you could never love anyone. You're all bottled up. You keep all your feelings all bottled up. And he could show his love. He could swish his tail and toss his head, and lick my hand when I gave him sugar. And late at night when I'd ride him bareback through the gray mountains ...
DAD. You never rode him — I just bought him ...
LISA. *(Music.)* You didn't know. I used to sneak out late at night when you thought I was sleeping. I'd climb out of my bedroom window and I'd run to the pasture ...
DAD. Pasture? What pasture?
LISA. And he'd smell my scent and come galloping toward me, and I'd leap onto his back, and we'd go galloping over the moon-

lit moor ...
DAD. Moonlit moor?
LISA. ... with the wind in my hair. And now he's dead. You killed my pony. You killed Black Thunder.
DAD. Black Thunder?
LISA. You killed the only thing I ever loved.
DAD. I didn't.
LISA. You did.
DAD. I didn't.
LISA. You did. You said you did. *(Music stops.)*
DAD. *(Blows party whistle.)* APRIL FOOL! *(Laughing.)*
LISA. April Fool? But, but it's not April, it's my birthday.
DAD. BIRTHDAY FOOL! *(Blows whistle, laughs.)*
LISA. You mean Black Thunder's not dead? Then who is under that blanket?
DAD. Not "who" but "what."
LISA. Wh-what? Wh-what's under there?
DAD. Three guesses.
LISA. I ... I don't know. You're cruel. You're the cruelest daddy in the whole world.
DAD. Three guesses.
LISA. A ... a candy bar?
DAD. Uh-uh.
LISA. A ... a turtle, a big gigantic turtle?
DAD. Nope, two down, one to go.
LISA. A ... a ... a rubber raft?
DAD. No ...
LISA. What then, what is it?
DAD. It's your sister!
LISA. What?
DAD. It's your big fat sister!
LISA. Cathy? It's Cathy?
DAD. Big fat Cathy!
LISA. Why is she hiding under there? And you said it was a what, not a who, Cathy is a who.
DAD. Not exactly.
LISA. Not exactly? Cathy? Ca — Cathy?
DAD. It's a ... what ... it's Cathy's body.

LISA. Cathy's body?
DAD. She's the one that bit me.
LISA. You shot Cathy?
DAD. Teeth like a damn wild grizzly.
LISA. You gave me my dead sister's body for a birthday present? First you tell me my pony is dead, and now you tell me you shot my favorite sister? You are the cruelest meanest most vicious ...
DAD. DOUBLE APRIL FOOL!! *(Blows whistle, laughs.)*
LISA. Double April Fool?
DAD. It's not your sister. I wouldn't shoot your fat little sister. Three more guesses!
LISA. *(Crying.)* I'm not guessing anymore. You ruined my birthday. You're a mean, cruel ...
DAD. It's the motorcycle you wanted!
LISA. The Honda?
DAD. Uh-huh.
LISA. The red one?
DAD. Uh-huh.
LISA. *(Screams.)* Really and truly?
DAD. Mmm-hmm.
LISA. No April Fool?
DAD. No.
LISA. No Birthday Fool's day?
DAD. Mmm-mmm.
LISA. Oh Daddy. *(Kisses him.)* Daddy, you're the bestest daddy in the whole wide world! *(Kisses, kisses, kisses.)*

THE LIFEBOAT IS SINKING

Jen and Sherwin sit in bed.

JEN. The waves are getting higher — thirty feet — *forty* feet — whitecaps — wind — *(Sound.)* The sea is screaming — we're taking on water — too much weight ... we're sinking — what do you

do? *(Sounds.)*
SHERWIN. I wait.
JEN. You can't wait. It's life or death. There is only food enough for three people. And no fresh water — just a few drops — I squeeze it into a handkerchief — the one you gave me for our anniversary — I squeeze out a few drops — Nancy cries "More water, Mommy" — Hush dear — Grandma needs a little water too —
SHERWIN. Jesus.
JEN. The waves — coming in — the boat's too heavy — we're sinking —
SHERWIN. *Life jackets!*
JEN. *No* life jackets — you forgot to bring them — we're sinking — too heavy. Somebody has to go overboard for the good of the others. What do you do?
SHERWIN. We may sight land.
JEN. We can't sight land. We're five hundred miles from land. What do you do? Somebody has to go. What choice do you make?
SHERWIN. We bail — we pitch in and we all —
JEN. All right — bail — bail — faster — faster — the water, it's — it's coming in too fast — Nancy's hands are tired — she cries — "Daddy, I'm tired — hold me, Daddy — Save me, Daddy."
SHERWIN. I bail faster — I bail all the water out of the goddamn —
JEN. *(Wave sound.)* Washed away — The bailing can is — washed right out of your hand — gone — "Help me, Daddy — I'm afraid" — She's saying, "Choose Daddy — please — make the decision. Choose." Wife, daughter or ... or ... mother.
SHERWIN. Where is *your* mother?
JEN. We'll do my mother later — *choose* — the waves are getting higher — the water is cold — the wind — the gulls screaming — choose — choose —
SHERWIN. Why are you doing this?
JEN. *We're* doing it — to find out — like we said we'd find out — all right? You agreed — so finish the game — the waves are crashing — Breaking — smashing — gulls screaming — the wind — Nancy is crying — "Help me, Da — "
SHERWIN. Stop saying Nancy is crying, stop trying to influence

me —
JEN. Well I'd be crying too — or bravely trying not to cry — I'd take Nancy in my arms — "Don't worry, baby — Daddy will find a way to — "
SHERWIN. Stop telling me what everybody is saying — stop trying to sway me with —
JEN. Sway you? Your wife and daughter are drowning and you —
SHERWIN. All right — and what is my mother saying? Let's have it all.
JEN. She's not saying anything — She doesn't *have* to say anything. She feels secure — she knows she's staying in the boat.
SHERWIN. If you know she's staying in the boat why *ask* me? — Why make me —
JEN. She *thinks* she's staying in the boat — nobody knows for sure — *You're* the one that knows — *You* have to decide — *Now* — *(Sounds.)*
SHERWIN. I can't — Okay? — I can't just —
JEN. Then we'll *all* die — all of us — is that what you want? — for all of us to drown?
SHERWIN. I don't want *anybody* to drown — I didn't want to even play this dumb fuckin' —
JEN. Then *choose* — save *two* of us — any two — but choose —
SHERWIN. *I* — Me — I go — I jump overboard — I *drown* — okay? Everybody's happy — I drown —
JEN. You *can't* — You're *needed* — to navigate — You're needed for navigation. You're the only one strong enough to throw one of us overboard —
SHERWIN. Why do *I* have to choose?
JEN. These are *your* people — we are all yours — *Your* wife — *Your* — daughter — *Your* mother — we're all tied together through you — *you! You* have to choose — *Now* — *Now* before we're all dead and drowned and just sightless, lifeless bloated corpses — floating to the bottom of the cruel and stormy sea ... *choose* — *(She continues ocean sounds.)* We're drowning — *(Gurgle.)* We're all ...
SHERWIN. I know what you want me to say, okay? You want me to say my *mother*. You ... want me to throw her into the sea — you *do* — You want me to ... visualize — throwing her into the

sea ... you want her to drown.

JEN. *Somebody* has to drown — that's the situation — somebody has to gurgle — and clutch and scream — but *who?* Choose *who* —

SHERWIN. I'll tell you what. My mother wouldn't let me choose. She'd *jump* over to save her grandchild.

JEN. And her son.

SHERWIN. That's right.

JEN. And her daughter-in-law? Ha.

SHERWIN. She'd jump.

JEN. Suppose she doesn't jump.

SHERWIN. She would.

JEN. She's not jumping. She's sitting there clinging to the side, clutching, drinking all the water and eating the biscuits.

SHERWIN. All by herself? She's the only one — You're not eating or drinking anything?

JEN. Okay, I'm eating too. And Nancy is eating. Do you mind that? If Nancy and I have a sip of water and bite of a soggy biscuit? Oh my God, there goes the biscuit — another wave — *Nancy* — grab her — hang on — hang on —

SHERWIN. You're tearing my heart out.

JEN. It's supposed to tear at your heart.

SHERWIN. Is that what you want to do? Tear me apart?

JEN. I want you to find out something. Admit something about yourself.

SHERWIN. What? *What?*

JEN. Crash — woosh — the water is rising — gurgle — Nancy is crying — "Help me, Daddy — save us. Daddy — Daddy — do *something* — "

SHERWIN. You are a cunt.

JEN. "Help! Daddy!" *(Gurgle.)*

SHERWIN. And you — what are *you* saying?

JEN. I'm saying *choose*. Choose *me* — Throw *me* — Even if you don't throw me — what will that prove? That you *love* me? Just that you need a mother for Nancy. That's all. So throw me — *throw me* —

SHERWIN. I can't throw you.

JEN. Throw me or throw *somebody* — or I swear — I'll jump — I will — *(She perches.)* — I've got Nancy in my arms — We'll both

jump — and sink from sight in the swirling froth — so you and your mother can sail away into the sunset.
SHERWIN. Don't start that "you and your" —
JEN. *(Perched.)* I'll jump — I'll count to three and then I *will* jump — I'll *leave* Nancy — I don't want to stack the deck — I'll leave Nancy crying "Mommy, Mommy" and I'll jump and you'll all be safe and you can all live together and eat a pot roast cooked by somebody who knows how to cook a pot roast and have your shirts ironed and live happily ever after — One — *(Poised.)* Two —
SHERWIN. You've got me crazy.
JEN. Throw me —
SHERWIN. *All right* — all right — *(He sobs.)*
JEN. *Choose* — *(Sounds.)*
SHERWIN. *All right.*
JEN. Who? Who? *(Louder sounds.)*
SHERWIN. *(Mumbling.)* My mother.
JEN. *Who?* I can't hear you —
SHERWIN. *My mother* — my *mother* —
JEN. Then *throw* her — throw her —
SHERWIN. I *told* you — she's the one I'd —
JEN. Don't tell me — *do* it — *do* it — *throw* her.
SHERWIN. *(Screams and grabs imaginary mother by arm and leg — flings her out of imaginary lifeboat into imaginary sea.)* AGGHH — MOMMA — Momma — *(He breaks down hysterically.)*
JEN. There — the boat is starting to right itself — we can bail now ... The storm is starting to subside —
SHERWIN. She's gone — gone — sunk into the waves — *(He cries.)* I'll never forgive you for making me go through this. All for a fucking game.
JEN. Calm down — you're distraught.
SHERWIN. Distraught? I've just thrown my own mother overboard to *save* your fucking ass. I've drowned my own mother in the fucking sea. All for your fucking game. Her clutching — hand, going down. Screaming — gurgling — with her last breath, "I love you all."
JEN. All?
SHERWIN. Yes, *all.* "You too, Jen. I love you too. I lo ... " *(Gurgle. Hand sinks. Sherwin gasps and trembles — he cries — he*

sobs.) Are you happy now — are you? *(Pause.)* You are — you're happy.
JEN. Happy? Happy? I just watched my own mother-in-law *drowned* — I watched her son — pick her up and heave her into the waves — My daughter saw it — Grandma — her Gama — we saw your pain — your anguish — how can we be happy? *(He cries.)* It wasn't easy … but it had to be done — it taught you something about your priorities — You understand something now — You've explored your feelings for your mother and for me and for Nancy. You've said something beautiful. "My mother, I'll drown my mother." That's horrible, but it's beautiful.
SHERWIN. Momma … Momma …
JEN. Shh — shh — the sea is quieting now — the skies clear — bright and blue — we sail into a bright sunset — the three of us — smooth sailing.
SHERWIN. Momma — Momma —
JEN. Shh — Nancy's sleeping — I've found some fresh biscuits — and water — fresh water — there *was* fresh water —
SHERWIN. There *was* fresh water. I just threw my own —
JEN. But you didn't know it — It was under the seat — so that Nancy could live — so she could have *her* momma — and her daddy.
SHERWIN. Sightless … Lifeless … Bloated …
JEN. Sherwin —
SHERWIN. Floating down — down — down … Hair spreading on the water … eyes staring …
JEN. It's past — the sea is quiet — and *there* — *land* — land ho!
SHERWIN. Where?
JEN. *There* — an island paradise — clear skies — *(Swaying.)* palm trees — gentle seas —
SHERWIN. Gentle seas —
JEN. And a happy family — sailing home — to port.
SHERWIN. Happy family —
JEN. Warm breezes —
SHERWIN. Sailing home —
JEN. To port. A man, his wife and his daughter — brought closer together by a — tragic experience.
SHERWIN. Closer together —

JEN. Yes. Calm and quiet seas — warm balmy breeze — bright clear skies — but wait — what's that?
SHERWIN. Huh?
JEN. On the horizon — that black spot —
SHERWIN. Wha — ?
JEN. Growing larger and larger — it's another typhoon —
SHERWIN. No!
JEN. *Thunder — lightning — the skies crashing — the gulls shrieking — Nancy is crying — the water is running low again — the biscuits — (Sherwin screams.)* Wait — hold on — don't panic. if you panic we're all lost. There's just enough for two people now. Just for two. Somebody's got to ...
SHERWIN. *NO GODDAMNIT, NO.*
JEN. *The waves — the thunder — sharks — oh my God, sharks — the boat — filled with water — too heavy — too heavy — the waves — thirty feet — crashing — smashing — forty feet — fifty feet — (Sherwin stares out in fear as the storm continues and lights fade.)*

SMILE

Bender sits on chair. Snooky and Jimbo drag Gibby in. Snooky pushes him into room.

SNOOKY. Get in there, you fuckin' sleaze bag. *(Gibby falls to knees.)*
BENDER. He's the one?
SNOOKY. Absolutely.
GIBBY. Please — I don't know what this is —
BENDER. Shut up. *(To Snooky.)* You're sure.
SNOOKY. Hey we found the *original* — show him, Jimbo. *(Jimbo unwraps large smile sign.)*
BENDER. You did this?
GIBBY. Please, I was just — *(Bender gets up and grabs his neck.)*
BENDER. Listen you little piece of shit — Don't tell me what

you were, when you were, how you were — answer what I ask you — you did this?
GIBBY. Yes — a long time ago ... yes — please, I've got to say something — I *drew* it — I didn't design it — there's a difference. Someone tells me what to draw — I draw it. I'm a draftsman — I'm not a creator — I don't have the imagination to create — a —
BENDER. You know what you remind me of? A fuckin' Nazi war criminal — Doesn't he remind you of a Nazi war criminal? "I only followed orders" — only you're *worse* than a Nazi — the Nazis just went after the Jews and the Poles — you got *everybody* — everybody is a little less because of you, you little fuck, and what did you get out of it? How much did they pay you, you fuckin' Judas? How much —
GIBBY. Twenty dollars ... really ... truly — I just did the design — I didn't manufacture it — twenty dollars I swear ... *(He sobs.)*
SNOOKY. And "Have a nice day."
BENDER. "Have a ... "
GIBBY. Please — the "have a nice day," that was part of the copy — they gave it to me — I just lettered it — please. *(He sobs.)*
BENDER. *Who* gave it to you? *(Grabs him.) Who gave you?*
GIBBY. He never gave his name ... just showed up at my studio. He had a rough sketch ... and the copy — "Have a nice day."
BENDER. And you just drew it — Some total stranger comes in with a thing like that and you just ... what kind of fuckin' animal are you? I should just blow you away like a fuckin' hog — step on you like a fuckin' cockaroach — "Have a nice day" — "Smile" *and* "Have a nice day."
JIMBO. They could only have been conceived by the same mind ... we got our guy.
GIBBY. It wasn't *my* mind — Please, I'm not a creative person *(He sobs.)*
BENDER. "*Smile*" and "Have a nice day" *(Gibby nods.)* — both for twenty dollars ... *(Gibby nods.)*
JIMBO. I don't believe it — not for one second — mysterious stranger — it's —
BENDER. I believe it — look at the pathetic little cunt — he couldn't invent anything. He couldn't merchandise anything.
JIMBO. Really? You think this is a coincidence? He just hap-

pened to be the ... what? *Draftsman* on this — eh? eh? He thinks that, Snooky ... surprise him.
BENDER. What?
SNOOKY. We found ... some papers ... in his desk.
BENDER. So?
SNOOKY. They ... link him —
BENDER. They link him ... with what? What do they link him with?
SNOOKY. "Far out."
BENDER. Jesus Christ. *(He covers eyes.)* "Far out" ...
JIMBO. And ... tell him the rest ...
SNOOKY. *(Pause.)* "Right on" ... *(Bender is shocked.)*
BENDER "Right on"? Right on?
JIMBO. We got more than we bargained for ...
SNOOKY. This will clear up four of the major ...
GIBBY. Mistake — it was a mistake — you say something — you say an innocent something — I'm out at the beach, somebody says, "Ohh look at that beautiful yacht," I say — "It's far out" — meaning — it's far out — there — in the middle of the lake — somebody else says "Yeah far out — isn't it far out?" Everybody says, "Yeah — FAAAR OUT — " I say, "Oh wow, don't start interpreting that as ... "
BENDER. *Oh wow?* Oh wow?
SNOOKY. We got ourselves a prize ...
BENDER. Oh wow?
JIMBO. We stepped in some deep shit — *Oh wow.*
GIBBY. Oh — *ow — ow —* they were slapping me on the back — it hurt — oh — *ow —*
BENDER. And for *"right on"*? Were they slapping your back for right on? Were they congratulating you for that monstrous piece of ...
GIBBY. The *words* — they misunderstood the words — *RIDE ON* — R-I-D-E — A bunch of Hell's Angels came into town — I wanted them out — I said *(Black fist.) RIDE ON — Ride on —* meaning ride out of here ...
BENDER. *(Fist?)* Eh?
GIBBY. I swung at them. *(Fist.)* RIDE ON out of here you biker bastards — You dirty greasy black jacket — piss-drinking greasy

hairy brown tooth sons of bitches — Haul your asses out of here — I need my own space — Get your goddamn —
JIMBO. "I need my own space"?
GIBBY. Something like that, words to that effect ...
JIMBO. We got the big fish.
BENDER. I think so.
SNOOKY. Should we ... send him far out? ... Give him his own space?
JIMBO. We've been waitin' a long time — It's gonna be a nice day. *(Jimbo and Snooky open switchblades and advance on Gibby.)*
GIBBY. Please ... please, it was so long ago. I was young, what did I know — these things came to me — they popped out of my head — like a poet — I couldn't stop it — I had to do my own thing. *(They wince.)* I never got credit for it — none of it — I never made a dime — Tim Leary got "Turn on Tune in Drop Out" — He got the cover of *Time* — I got shit — Okay I did some bad things — "Sex and Drugs and Rock and Roll" that was bad — I admit it — "Don't trust anybody over thirty." *(They wince.)*
BENDER. You're responsible for ...
GIBBY. What did I know? I was under thirty — I never learned to trust people. I learned — I learned to trust — people — over thirty — yes — yes — Okay — I got caught up ... You know young people — I'd say something like ... "Paul lives" — the next day everybody in the Haight-Ashbury was saying it — in two days — the whole country was on it — A week later it's on the Carson show — They didn't even let me finish — what I started to say was, "Paul lives in London" — they wouldn't wait — took it and ran with it — I was — my ego was all blown up — I was a kid — you don't blame Elvis for what he did as a kid — Jimi Hendrix? Janis — if I wasn't into drugs — I wasn't hurting anybody — I wasn't bad — But I learned — I did *good* things too — "Make Love Not War," that was mine — *(They advance on him.)* — that was *mine* — "Hell no we won't go" — "Bombs are bad for children and flowers and other living things" — I did that — I drew the daisy — "Don't give a dose to the one you love most"? — I learned — I became responsible — "Black is beautiful." I'm not black — But I did it — "You can't hug your children with nuclear arms"? Didn't you see that? Didn't anybody see that — That was

30

mine — Not to worry — that's my latest — Not to worry ... *(They advance on him.)* Not to worry?
BENDER. Smile ... Right on ... Have a nice ...
SNOOKY. My own space ...
JIMBO. Right on. Right on — Right on ...
GIBBY. I was young — please — It was so long ago — so long ago ...
BENDER. Did you think we'd forget? Those of us who were there ... Did you think we'd forget? *(Lights fade.)*

WASH AND DRY

The laundromat. George sits and waits. Marianne enters with laundry bag.

MARIANNE. *(Entering.)* Good morning. *(She puts bag on counter.)*
GEORGE. Good morning.
MARIANNE. It's a beautiful morning — *(She rummages in purse for ticket.)*
GEORGE. It's in the eye of the beholder. Wash and dry?
MARIANNE. Yes. Thank you. It's a fresh brisk morning. *(Still looking for ticket.)*
GEORGE. *(Weighing.)* You know how many fresh brisk mornings there have been in the world? Millions — hundreds of millions — and what good has it done? Five forty-three.
MARIANNE. Well it's cool and crisp and not a cloud in the sky — all you can see are blue skies — *(She pays.)*
GEORGE. If I can see blue skies it's not a beautiful day — you know what's a beautiful day? When I can't see any skies at all — when those laundry bags are piled so high you can't see the sky at all — that's what I call a beautiful day — *(He takes bag.)*
MARIANNE. Here's my ticket — I usually lose the ticket. I feel very proud of myself for having it.
GEORGE. Don't be so proud of yourself. You know how many

lost laundry tickets there've been in the world? Hundreds of thousands — hundreds of thousands of people saying, "I seem to have lost my ticket," and hundreds of thousands of laundry owners saying, "Well, you'll have to sign for it" — and hundreds of thousands of — customers lying — "I never got a ticket" — hundreds of laundry owners saying, "You did get a ticket — I gave you a ticket — where is your ticket? Where is — ?"
MARIANNE. I *have* my ticket — the sun is shining and I have my laundry ticket.
GEORGE. *(Reading.)* Twelve-oh-seven — *(She looks around.)*
MARIANNE. That's it up there, the blue bag.
GEORGE. All the way up there.
MARIANNE. The blue bag with the rope string. It matches this one.
GEORGE. Well?
MARIANNE. Well? It's mine.
GEORGE. Well, nobody's saying it isn't yours. Who's saying it isn't yours?
MARIANNE. Well, may I have it please?
GEORGE. Sure you can have it. It's yours.
MARIANNE. May I have it *now* — why not now — Well?
GEORGE. Go get it.
MARIANNE. Go get it?
GEORGE. Why not? It's yours, isn't it?
MARIANNE. I should go get it?
GEORGE. Watch your step climbin' up there — don't step on the top rung — it's rickety — I can't be responsible if you step on that top rung.
MARIANNE. Why don't *you* get it?
GEORGE. Ha-ha. That's a very good question. You want a very good answer — I don't get it because I don't *have* to get it — I didn't agree to get it — wash and dry — not wash, dry and get.
MARIANNE. Getting it — is — just part of the service — it's *expected.*
GEORGE. By you.
MARIANNE. By anyone — It's expected that when you pick up your —
GEORGE. Don't expect too much of life — you'll be sorely dis-

illusioned — you're talking to somebody who knows — don't expect a bed of roses.
MARIANNE. A bed of roses? It's just a common courtesy — it's only —
GEORGE. I did not promise wash, dry and courtesy, did I?
MARIANNE. Obviously not.
GEORGE. Well then, I'm not guilty of false advertising, am I? Am I?
MARIANNE. You're really not going to get it.
GEORGE. Wash and dry, period. *(He reads newspaper.)*
MARIANNE. Well — I'll tell you something — *(She begins to climb.)* You don't know how to run a business.
GEORGE. You get what you're promised — consider yourself lucky — most of the time we don't even get what we're promised.
MARIANNE. *(Pulling laundry down.)* Oops.
GEORGE. I warned you about that ladder, didn't I? I warned you loud and clear — I said it's rickety.
MARIANNE. I'll tell you something else. I'm not coming back here anymore.
GEORGE. Never say never — We don't know what we'll do — circumstances — change.
MARIANNE. And ... And if I hadn't paid for this in advance, I wouldn't pay for it now.
GEORGE. Oh, I know that — and that's exactly why I collect in advance — *exactly* why.
MARIANNE. And you'd better not have shrunk my blue cotton blouse — *(She rummages through bag.)* I distinctly said — no hot water —
GEORGE. No hot water was used — it's not shrunk.
MARIANNE. It better not be.
GEORGE. I guarantee it.
MARIANNE. *(Pulling blouse out.)* God.
GEORGE. Well —
MARIANNE. It — it's not even —
GEORGE. I told you.
MARIANNE. It hasn't been — *washed* — it's still — it's just like it was when I brought it in —
GEORGE. No shrinkage — a promise made, a promise fulfilled

33

— but don't get *used* to that — don't start expecting that in the rest of your beautiful day —
MARIANNE. It's all — they're all — still dirty. These clothes have *not* been washed. You make me climb up and risk my neck to get my own laundry that you forgot to wash —
GEORGE. I didn't forget. You don't stay in business by forgetting.
MARIANNE. You didn't forget? You just did not —
GEORGE. You get what you contracted for.
MARIANNE. What I contracted for? I contracted for dirty clothes? I brought them in here to be washed and dried — I *contracted* for —
GEORGE. *Watched.*
MARIANNE. What?
GEORGE. *Watched* — not washed. Watch and dry.
MARIANNE. *Watched?*
GEORGE. George's *Watch* and Dry. *(Sign.)* You gotta pay attention — They'll rob you blind. They'll take the gold fillings out of your teeth.
MARIANNE. George's Watch and Dry?
GEORGE. They count on the fact that people don't pay attention — they *depend* on that.
MARIANNE. I paid five dollars and forty-three cents to have my clothes *watched?*
GEORGE. And dried.
MARIANNE. But you haven't *washed* them.
GEORGE. I've *watched* them. I've been watching them for five days —
MARIANNE. Why would somebody want to have their clothes *watched?* Why?
GEORGE. Why is a goose not a gander? There's lots of strange people in this town — bizarre people with unusual needs — and desires. I don't ask questions — They want watch and dry, they get watch and dry.
MARIANNE. I did not come here to have my clothes *watched*. I did not pay five dollars and forty-three cents to have my clothes *watched*.
GEORGE. And dry.
MARIANNE. Of course they're dry. They've never been wet. I

paid to — have my clothes *washed* — *washed*.
GEORGE. You should have taken them to a laundromat.
MARIANNE. I thought this was a laundromat. That's why I —
GEORGE. Marianne — Marianne — don't agitate yourself.
MARIANNE. You know my name?
GEORGE. I'm not like some people. I care. I pay attention. Read the small print — if you don't they'll skin you alive — they'll peel you like a grape.
MARIANNE. *You're* peeling me like a grape — you're charging me —
GEORGE. I'm teaching you — you've got to —
MARIANNE. Teaching me? By charging me five dollars and forty-three cents to *watch* my clothes? You think that's teaching?
GEORGE. If the lesson was free, you wouldn't learn it.
MARIANNE. I assume you're not giving me my money back.
GEORGE. This is not George's *free* Watch and Dry —
MARIANNE. Well, I'm going to the police — directly — I'm going to the Better Business Bureau and they are going to be all over you like a rash. I am not one of those people who suffer in silence. I do not get fleeced silently — I'm not a sheep. I get raped and I *identify* the rapist. I hunt *him* down and see him prosecuted and punished —
GEORGE. I'm only teaching you what they taught me — I'm passing on the information.
MARIANNE. Information? That people will take your money on a technicality — for watching your laundry — what kind of information is that?
GEORGE. It's real information — all the love thy neighbor — do unto others — sisters and brothers stuff — that's all *mis*information — you know what they did to me? They guaranteed my color TV — at least I *thought* they guaranteed it — I assumed — I assumed that was what I was paying three hundred and eighty-five dollars for — and then when the tube blew — then and only then did they inform me that it was not a guarantee — but a *warranty* — that's when they told me to read the fine print.
MARIANNE. Your color TV has nothing to do with —
GEORGE. That was the beginning of my education — my transmission was another lesson — my electrical wiring was another

lesson — and my reupholstery — *and* my Blue Cross — oh, they've taught me a lesson or two — That's when I started paying attention — that's when I started passing along the information.
MARIANNE. That's when you started watching clothes.
GEORGE. Yes, as matter of fact.
MARIANNE. For five dollars and forty-three cents.
GEORGE. Two fifty a load — plus tax.
MARIANNE. A load? Of what? What load.
GEORGE. A machine load.
MARIANNE. Which never goes into the machine.
GEORGE. It's a measurement — You've got to pay attention — Because something is a machine load doesn't mean it *gets* into a machine. Are you beginning to comprehend?
MARIANNE. I comprehend that you have charged me five dollars and forty-three cents to watch — my laundry — and there's not proof that you have even watched it. I *am* going to the police — I really am —
GEORGE. Go ahead, go to the police — And try to prove I didn't watch your stupid laundry — and I'll tell you something else, sweetheart — of all the laundry I ever watched, yours was the most bizarre —
MARIANNE. Bizarre? My laundry was — ?
GEORGE. Item — chocolate stains on nightgown —
MARIANNE. Chocolate stains?
GEORGE. Or hot fudge — Who am I to say? — I'm no goddamn chemist — and butterscotch stains on nightgown, denoting late night —
MARIANNE. You *looked* through my laundry —
GEORGE. I *watched* your laundry — you want more proof? Item stains on *blouse* — denoting early day dieting and late-night loss of willpower — also sloppy eating, I might add.
MARIANNE. Sloppy eating — you're judging my — ?
GEORGE. Item — wine stains on slacks, denoting heavy drinking and possible alcoholism.
MARIANNE. Alcoholi —
GEORGE. Or *potential* alcoholism — Item — one white capsule — possibly Nembutal — in pocket of —
MARIANNE. Possibly *what?*

GEORGE. Or it might be an aspirin — How would I know? That's for the boys in the lab to figure out.
MARIANNE. What boys? What lab?
GEORGE. That's for me to know and you to find out. If it turns out to be an aspirin, you have my apology — but if it turns out to be a Nembutal — I'd say cut out the booze — It's a dangerous combination. Item — One pair of pantyhose — *one* pair — two weeks' laundry — four sets of sheets and pillowcases and only one pair of pantyhose. Leaving owner's personal hygiene in question.
MARIANNE. You — you count my sheets and my —
GEORGE. And upon two of those sheets — a dried white residue — possibly semen — I say possibly — possibly dried rubber cement — possibly semen — possibly indicating a certain sexual promiscuity —
MARIANNE. I can't believe —
GEORGE. Item — blood stains on underwear and white skirt, denoting unusually heavy menstrual flow and possibly due to recent dilation and curettage. *(Marianne gasps — sobs, whimpers, stammers.)* Don't get yourself agitated — learn your lesson — epileptics have to be careful — *fill* your prescription — *(He unfolds it.)* Don't leave it in your pocket — stay on your medication — don't get agitated. Don't spend time with men who give you ... problems.
MARIANNE. How would you like your neck broken? Really — my boyfriend — I could tell him what you're — he's a big guy — he is — he could just break your little neck — how would you like that?
GEORGE. How would his wife like that? — Your big guy — *(Takes shirt.)* Eighteen-inch neck, thirty-six sleeve — initials V.R. — V.R. — Vincent Romo? — Dispatcher control at United? — Eh? — V.R.? I think we may have the mystery man here.
MARIANNE. Mystery man?
GEORGE. Possibly the donor of said semen — *or* said rubber cement — possibly the reason for said alcoholism — and said compulsive overeating — possibly — of course, if your father or brother's initials are V.R. — then there's no problem — but that is highly doubtful since your mother's initials are R.D. — unless, of course, she married again, in which case —

MARIANNE. *My mother?*
GEORGE. *(Reading letter.)* Mrs. Donovan, 623 Lake Terrace Road, Milwaukee, Wisconsin? You should answer her letters — she would like some news of you — some news — 623 Lake Terrace Road — it sounds like a nice street — they've put in some poplar trees across from the Hanleys' place — but she doesn't think they'll take —
MARIANNE. I know what it says — give it to me — *(She grabs the letter.)* That's my property.
GEORGE. Hey, it's *yours* — you've got a right to it — 623 Lake Terrace Road, I think the zip is four-oh-oh-five — but I could look it up
MARIANNE. You could look it up —
GEORGE. If I wanted to — If I chose to — you don't control the postal service, you know — I can write to whom I choose — I don't need a warrant to write to whom I choose — I'm free to —
MARIANNE. You — You cannot do this — You cannot violate a person's life — by prying into their laundry — Listen, my father happens to be a very prominent attorney in Milwaukee — I happen to know something about the law — do you realize what you're perpetrating? Breach of contract — charging me for services not recei —
GEORGE. W-A-T-C-H — clearly stated — W-A-T —
MARIANNE. Invasion of privacy — going through my —
GEORGE. Hey, I *have* to handle — that's part of my —
MARIANNE. Slander — accusing me of —
GEORGE. I'm not accusing — *this* is accusing — Item — small white powdery residue in front of blue wool sweater — possibly cocaine — possibly face powder — I'm not a goddamn criminologist — call 'em in and we'll settle the question — *Your* property? — Hey, it's none of my business, it's your business — Possibly American Airlines might think it's *their* business — but I —
MARIANNE. Go ahead — tell them — Just *try* to tell them. Tell them I —
GEORGE. I won't tell 'em, I'll show 'em.
MARIANNE. Show them what? — *This* — *(Grabs it — George shows Polaroids.)* You took ... *Polaroids* ... of my — *(Reaches.)*
GEORGE. Uh-uh — *my* property — to substantiate my claim —

that I watched — you question whether I really watched — You cast aspersions on my professional integrity — Okay, I got proof — I watch —

MARIANNE. You are a rotten, vicious — perverted —

GEORGE. I pay attention — the police pay attention — I'm trying to teach you to pay attention — *watch* and dry — *watch* and dry — read the small print. *(Marianne begins to walk out slowly with laundry.)* Will I be hearing from your father? Your big boyfriend? Will I be seeing you in court? … Next Tuesday then.

MARIANNE. Next Tuesday — ?

GEORGE. Before four o'clock — I close at four on Tuesday.

MARIANNE. You think I'd *ever* bring my laundry in here again — to be watched — to be — violation — a breach of contract — What's legal? What's illegal? *(He fingers vial with cocaine sample — Marianne stops.)* Okay then — *(He takes pencil.)* I'll put you down for an eight-pound load on Wednesday — every Wednesday — *(Marianne bites her lip and leaves.)* You got to read the small print — they'll squeeze you like an orange — Don't think they won't — Don't assume anything — Pay attention, for God's sake — *(He sits back down and opens newspaper. Marianne exits, in shock.)* And let's not wait two weeks on the pantyhose — eh?

KENNETH. *(Entering with laundry.)* Hi —

GEORGE. Put it on the scale.

KENNETH. *(Putting it on scale.)* Can I get this back before the weekend?

GEORGE. No problem. Six dollars and twenty-five cents.

KENNETH. *(Paying.)* Oh, and no starch, please.

GEORGE. Okay.

KENNETH. And I can get it back by Friday? For sure?

GEORGE. Just watch and dry?

KENNETH. Yes.

GEORGE. I guarantee it. *(He turns back to newspaper as the curtain falls.)*

THINKING UP A NEW NAME FOR THE ACT

Act I

> *Lucy and Pete in kitchen. He wears a straw hat. Another straw hat hangs from the back of her chair. He sits at the table scribbling on a pad. She stands at stove stirring pot. He mouths ideas silently. He scribbles more. She brings pot to table.*

LUCY. Meat? *(No response — he scribbles.)* Meat? *(He looks up absently, nods — she puts meat on his plate.)* Potatoes? *(He grunts — she puts potatoes on his plate and starts to serve herself.)*
PETE. *(Bored with food.)* Meat 'n' potatoes, meat 'n' potatoes, meat 'n' ... *(Brainstorm.)* Potatoes — *meat and potatoes* — *(He leaps up.)* meat and potatoes. Meat and potatoes — *(She stares at him, confused.)* Meat — *(He points to himself.)* and — *(He points to her.)* potatoes — meat meets potatoes ... potatoes meet meat — "MMM meat," "MMM potatoes — " *(Shake hands — imaginary marquee.)* meat and *potatoes* ... *(He grabs straw hat — announcing.)* Meat and *potatoes* — *(Applause — he puts her hat on her, gets behind her and starts shufflin' off to Buffalo — she resists but dances uncomfortably — he smiles — sings to tune of "There's No Business Like Show Business.")*
    Meet *meat* and po-ta-toes
    Meet meat ... and po-ta-toes
    Meat meat meat meat meat meat meat meat,
    potatoes
    Meat meat meat meat meat ... po-ta-toes-toes
    Meat meat meat meat meat meat meat meat meat meat meat
    Meet meat and potatoes. *(Applause.)* Meat — *(He does wild solo.)* Potatoes — *("Take it" — she doesn't move.)* Potatoes — *(She won't dance.)* Po-ta-toes — *(Wants her to shake her tits.)* Potatoes — *(She looks coldly.)* Meat — *(Him.)* Potatoes *(Her.)*

LUCY. Meat and — *(Marquee.)* potatoes?
PETE. *(Nods, smiling.)* Meat and potatoes.
LUCY. *(Shakes her head no — marquee.) Potatoes — and meat. (She smiles — she starts to slow dance, humming "No business ... ")*
PETE. *Potatoes* and *meat? (She nods, still dancing.)* Potatoes and meat? *(He giggles.)* Potatoes and meat — *(He laughs — she stops — he looks cold and serious.) Meat ...* and *potatoes. (He begins dancing again — she is distressed — he, macho.)* Meat — *(Delicate — pointing to her.)* potatoes. Meat and potatoes. *(She is disturbed — he grabs his dick.)* Meat — *(Tweaks her nipples.)* and potatoes, Meat and potatoes.
LUCY. *(Slapping her own ass.)* Meat and — *(Pinching his balls.)* Potatoes. Meat and potatoes, meat and potatoes, meat and potatoes.
PETE. *(Angry — grabs dick.)* Meat.
LUCY. *(Smiling.)* Meat? Meat? — ha-ha — Meat.
PETE. *(Her tits.)* Potatoes — *(Grabs dick.)* Meat.
LUCY. *(Ass.)* Meat — *(Tits.)* meat ... and *(Diminutive points to balls.)* po-ta-toes.
PETE. *(Big balls — King Kong.)* Potatoes.
LUCY. *(Teenie weenie balls.)* Potatoes.
PETE. *(Grabs her — points to dick.) Meat — meat —*
LUCY. Potatoes — *(She laughs.)*
PETE. Potatoes? Potatoes? *(He starts to unzip pants.)*
LUCY. *(In feigned awe.)* Ooh, *meat ...* and *potatoes. (She laughs.)*
PETE. *(Grabs her arm and twists it.)* Meat.
LUCY. Pot-atoes.
PETE. *(Twisting.)* Meat.
LUCY. *(In pain but not giving in.)* Potatoes.
PETE. *(Hurting her.)* Meat — *(Twists more.)* Meat? — *(Twists.)* Meat — *(Twists.)*
LUCY. *(Crying, anger.) Potatoes — Potatoes — Potatoes —*
PETE. Meat? *(Silence.)* Meat?
LUCY. *(Finally giving up.)* Meat.
PETE. *(His dick.)* Meat?
LUCY. *(Whispers.)* Meat.
PETE. *(Macho.)* Meat.
LUCY. *(Macho.)* Meat.
PETE. *(Her tits.)* Potatoes?
LUCY. *Potatoes, potatoes — (She starts to sob, he releases her, she*

continues to cry.)
PETE. Meat and potatoes ... Meat and potatoes? *(She doesn't answer — pause — he tries to charm her.)* Potatoes? *(Touches her tit — she pulls away.)* Meat? *(Points to dick.)* Meat and potatoes? *(No response — points to her crotch.)* Meat? ... and — *(His balls.)* potatoes? — *(No response.)* Meat? *(Her ass.)* And — *(Diminutive — balls.)* potatoes? Potatoes? — *(He makes licking gesture.)* Meat — *(He grabs his dick and makes biting gestures.)* Meat meat meat meat meat meat meat — *(No response — he gets behind her and starts to dance and sing romantically.)*
    Meat and potatoes la-la-la
    Meat and potatoes la-la-la
    Meat and potatoes la-la-la
    Potatoes and meat.
LUCY. *(Her fist.)* Meat and — *(Punches him in balls.)* potatoes, potatoes, potatoes — *(He falls to his knees.)* Potatoes? *(She picks out one and bounces it off him.)* Meat? *(She takes pot and pours some over him.)* Meat and potatoes — *(Bows.)* Meat — *(Introducing him.)* and *potatoes* — *(Curtsy — applause — she grabs straw hat and jams it on.)* Meat — *(Her ass.)* potatoes — *(Her tits.)* Potatoes, potatoes — *(She grabs his hat and starts to dance off.)*
    Meat and potatoes
    Potatoes and meat —
(She dances off, doing a single and singing, one hat fanning ass, one hat fanning tits.)
    Meat and potatoes
    Meat and potatoes —
(He stares after her — he rises unsteadily to his feet, he sits at table as her singing fades away. He stares straight ahead dejectedly — he picks up fork sadly and begins to eat meat and potatoes — as lights fade.)

Act II

Pete lies dead under cloth. Inspector and Sergeant investigate.

INSPECTOR. *(Picks up piece of meat.)* Meat.
SERGEANT. *(Makes note of it.)* Meat.
INSPECTOR. And ... potatoes.
SERGEANT. *(Scribbling.)* Potato.
INSPECTOR. Potat*oes*.
SERGEANT. Pota-*toes*.
INSPECTOR. *(Thinking.)* Meat and potatoes ... hmm ... meat — *(He examines piece of meat — he smells it — he puts it down.)* potatoes — *(He picks one up — he tastes it — shrugs.)* potatoes ... Meat and potatoes.
SERGEANT. *(Goes to Pete's body, pulls back sheet, reaches under Pete's head and lifts red drippy brains.)* Meat. *(He hands out brains to Inspector, who takes them gingerly.)*
INSPECTOR. Meat — *(Disgusted — he looks around — he notices plant in pot — he walks to it — examines plant — lifts pot.)* Mmm — *(He removes something from bottom of pot.)* Meat — *(He compares it with brain meat.)* Meat ... and ... *(He lifts up Lucy's hat and two potatoes roll out.)* potatoes. *(He smiles in satisfaction as lights fade.)*

Act III

The courtroom. Judge sits. Prosecutor stands. Bailiff calls.

BAILIFF. Potatoes ... potatoes. *(Lucy steps to witness stand.)* Potatoes? *(She nods — he motions for her to sit — she does.)*

PROSECUTOR. *(Approaches her melodramatically — reaching behind back, he produces piece of meat.)* Meat? *(He extends it to her — she looks at it indifferently — he extends it further — it smells.)* Meat?
LUCY. *(Casually.)* Meat.
PROSECUTOR. *(Produces straw hat with potatoes in it.)* Potatoes?
LUCY. Potatoes ... Meat and potatoes. *(So what?)*
PROSECUTOR. And ... *(He produces pot.)* meat — *(Throws meat in pot.)* Potatoes — *(Throws potatoes in pot.)* Meat and potatoes —
LUCY. *(Slowly goes mad — she tells her story beginning with the cooking, getting wilder and faster as she goes. Cooking.)* Meat and potatoes, meat and potatoes — *(Weary.)* Meat and potatoes — *(His ideas.) Meat* — and potatoes — *(Me.)* Potatoes — *(Him.)* meat — *(Dance.)* meat and potatoes, meat and potatoes — *(Stops.) Potatoes* and meat. *(Him.)* Potatoes and *meat? (He laughs.)* Potatoes and meat? *(Laugh — gets mean.)* Meat and potatoes — *(Her.) Potatoes* and meat — *(He.) Meat* and potatoes — *(Twists arm.)* Meat and potatoes — *(She, grimacing.)* Potatoes and meat — *(He — more violent.)* Meat and *potatoes* — *(She, giving in.)* Meat-and-potatoes — meat and potatoes — *(Him laughing.)* Meat — *(He grabs crotch.)* and potatoes — *(Tits — her surprised.)* Potatoes? Potatoes? *(She covers breasts — he — lecherous — holds dick.)* Meat-meat-meat-meat-meat-meat-meat — *(Squeezing, licking.)* Potatoes-potatoes-potatoes — *(She points to his dick.)* Meat? *(Holds her breasts.) Meat* and *potatoes* — *Meat* and *potatoes* — *(Grabs pot handle.) Meat* — *(Swings pot.) potatoes* — *(Swings.)* Meat — *(Swings.)* potatoes — *(Swings.)* Meat-potatoes-meat-potatoes-meat-potatoes-meat — *(She keeps swinging pot and babbling until she collapses — she sobs, head in hands.)*
JUDGE. *(Sadly summing up.)* Meat ... and potatoes. *(Lights fade.)*

Act IV

The execution room of Folsom Prison. Executioner stands by electric chair switch. Lucy enters flanked by two guards. Clergyman follows, reading text. He mumbles almost inaudibly.

CLERGYMAN. Meat and potatoes, potatoes, potatoes, meat meat meat meat meat potatoes meat meat meat meat ... pota-toes ... *(Guard sits Lucy in chair — they strap her in. The executioner throws the switch — Lucy stiffens, then goes limp.)*
FIRST GUARD. *(Sniffing.)* Meat? *(Executioner nods.)*
SECOND GUARD. *(Sniffing.)* Meat.
EXECUTIONER. ... and ... *(Reaches under Lucy.)* potatoes — *(He comes up with three steaming, foil-wrapped baked potatoes — they start to eat them with gusto as the curtain falls.)*

BUY ONE, GET ONE FREE

Merrilee and Sherilee, two street hookers. They hold sign that says, "Buy one, get one free." People pass. The girls wait. They sing.

BOTH. Buy one, get one free.
SHERILEE. Buy her, we'll throw in me.
MERRILEE. It's a steal.
SHERILEE. It's the deal of the century.
MERRILEE. Buy one — get one free — ee —
BOTH. Buy one — get one free —
MERRILEE. That "Buy one, get one free" — is that — what it seems to be?

SHERILEE. Hi — I'm Sherilee.
MERRILEE. Hi — I'm Merrilee.
BOTH. And it's an absolute money-back guarantee.
SHERILEE. Enjoy our hospitality. And in the utmost privacy. The thought you harbor inwardly. Will be performed ...
MERRILLE. *Artistically.* Any secret fantasy ...
SHERILEE. Any ... eccentricity?
MERRILEE. Any ... abnormality?
SHERILEE. Like — whips?
MERRILEE. Or bestiality?
SHERILEE. Any dark perversity? Some masochistic tendency?
MERRILEE. Some act of harsh brutality?
SHERILEE. A fantasy of chastity — *(Pose.)*
MERRILEE. Virginity — *(Pose.)*
SHERILEE. Timidity — *(Pose.)*
MERRILEE. Some fetish we can ...
SHERILEE. Like six-inch heels — *(Shows.)*
MERRILEE. Or lingerie — *(Shows.)*
SHERILEE. Someone we should pretend to be?
MERRILEE. Your mama? *(Pose.)*
SHERILEE. Daughter? *(Pose.)*
MERRILEE. A *she* ... or a *he* — *(Moustache.)*
SHERILEE. Some special words to shake your tree? *(Whispers.)*
MERRILEE. Some special sight you'd like to see — *(Both pose.)*
SHERILEE. Some special place you'd like to pee?
MERRILEE. All in the lap of luxury. *(They mime.)*
SHERILEE. A cup of tea?
MERRILEE. Some chilled chablis?
SHERILEE. A fresh croissant?
MERRILEE. A slice of brie?
SHERILEE. A tempting, glowing, overflowing, frosty frozen daiquiri?
MERRILEE. *Or —* if you live adventurously —
SHERILEE. Some P.C.P.?
MERRILEE. Some T.H.C.?
SHERILEE. Some hot — erot — photography? *(Pose.)*
MERRILEE. Shall we anoint you bodily?
SHERILEE. With — mayonnaise?

MERRILEE. Or sea and ski?
SHERILEE. Shall we dress up? Pretend to be your mama? Your daughter? Or sister Ann Marie?
MERRILEE. Just say her name, I'll be she.
SHERILEE. Whisper his name and I'll be he.
MERRILEE. Let us probe your — memory
 For some special thought we can set free?
SHERILEE. Some special sight — you'd like to see? *(Pose.)*
MERRILEE. Some special place — you'd like to pee?
SHERILEE. You'll find in Merrilee and me
 No sugary insincerity
 No crass commerciality
 No crudeness —
MERRILEE. No vulgarity
 No dimly-veiled hostility
 In our soft-lit facility
 In incense-filled tranquility
 You'll witness durability.
SHERILEE. *And* our extreme agility. *(Stretch.)*
MERRILEE. We say in all due modesty
BOTH. We'll take you on an odyssey ... if you —
 Buy one, you get one free.
MERRILEE. Try *me* —
SHERILEE. And get a gift of me —
MERRILEE. It's the deal of —
SHERILEE. The steal of —
MERRILEE. The century.
BOTH. Buy one — get one free — ee — ee
 Buy one and get one free.
SHERILEE. In half-priced — tax-free — gaiety
 And joyous spontaneity.
MERRILEE. We'll be thrilled to feel and see
 Your great desirability. *(They wind 'round him.)*
SHERILEE. Your animal *virility.*
MERRILEE. Your manly *electricity.*
SHERILEE. But — if there's some ... incapability —
MERRILEE. Some fear — of infertility?
SHERILEE. Some childlike timidity?

47

MERRILEE. Some frigid unrigidity?
SHERILEE. Some physical deformity?
MERRILEE. No matter the enormity.
SHERILEE. We'll meet it with our empathy.
MERRILEE. And treat it with our sympathy.
SHERILEE. And with our love capacity
　　For all your incapacity.
MERRILEE. And our dogged tenacity.
SHERILEE. T'will lead to love's discovery.
MERRILEE. And your complete recovery.
SHERILEE. The girls view you indifferently?
MERRILEE. We'll strengthen you magnificently.
　　Your sweetheart treats you viciously?
SHERILEE. We'll comfort you — deliciously.
　　Your wife is Ms. Frigidity?
　　I'm heat —
MERRILEE. And I'm *humidity*.
SHERILEE. Just think how it will be to see
　　Two bodies moving gracefully.
MERRILEE. Lovingly. Dreamily.
SHERILEE. Undulating endlessly.
MERRILEE. In orchestrated symmetry. *(Harmony.)*
SHERILEE. Don't miss this opportunity.
MERRILEE. To see us love in unity.
LEE. You and me? *(Nod.)*
　　Me and she? *(Nod.)*
　　She and — thee? *(Nod.)*
　　Then all *three?*
BOTH. In ecstasy —
LEE. Ooh-ooohee — that soliloquy
　　Struck to the very soul of me
　　But now speaking confidentially
　　How much will this love cost — eventually
　　But now speaking financially
　　How much will it be — in *greenery?*
SHERILEE. A C.
MERRILEE. One *C.*
SHERILEE. One teenie little C.

MERRILEE. A safe investment — and tax-free.
SHERILEE. A *C*.
MERRILEE. One *C* — that's practically free.
  For a double entrée, like she and me.
SHERILEE. One C for an hour — one lousy *C* —
MERRILEE. And of course, any small gratuity
  Will be remembered till perpetuity.
LEE. A *C*? One *C*, one little bitty *C*?
  I think somebody's tryin' to flim-flam me
  You think I got the mentality
  Of some tourist hick from Tennessee
  Who got off the bus at half-past three?
  I spend a *C* and what the hell's free
  That's just as much as anything would be.
SHERILEE. *Two* for a C? — of this quality?
MERRILEE. You must be out of your friggin' tree
  You want somethin' *here* substantially —
SHERILEE. You gotta put somethin' *here* financially.
LEE. You double the price originally
  Then you hype up the commodity
  With a lot of sweet banalities
  To play upon our vanities
  All that "double electricity"
  Ain't nothin' but duplicity
  You're banking on the culpability
  Of the uneducated community
  And you do it with impunity
  But that don't work with a dude like me
  A holder of a Ph.D. degree
  From an Ivy League university
  Where I majored in economy.
SHERILEE. *So* — our warmth and generosity
  Is met with animosity. *(She cries.)*
MERRILEE. *You* — you have the temerity
  To question *our* sincerity
  Where is your sense of chivalry
  Have you no shred of decency
  To speak so disrespectfully

>   To two sweet creatures such as we
>   Two pillars of the community
>   Who have contributed significantly
>   To this community's economy
>   Both holders of Ph.D. degrees.
> SHERILEE. In phys. ed. and economy — *(Cries again.)*
> MERRILEE. From a small Midwestern university
>   And whose father is a rich M.D.
>   Back home in Schenectady
>   Two women of sincerity
>   And proven popularity.
> SHERILEE. And the closest thing to virginity
>   You'll find in this vicinity.
> MERRILEE. You have the effrontery
>   To say these things in front of me
>   A man of your *obesity*
>   And grating personality
>   Bad breath, incapability
>   And latent homosexuality
>   Verging on senility
>   You doubt *our* credibility.
> LEE. Hey, cool that animosity
>   I just expressed some ... curiosity
>   I wasn't asking for no charity
>   I just was trying to bring some clarity — *(He touches Sherilee's arm.)*
> SHERILEE. Get your paws off of me please —
>   Money talks and bullshit flees
>   So take your nickel and dime mentality
>   To some more receptive locality
>   Bye-bye — begone as you can be
>   You're blockin' the product so the buyers can't see. *(View.)*
> LEE. Hey, stop spittin' your venom at me
>   Or I'll kick your ass a time or three.
> MERRILEE. *You'll* kick ass — you little flea
>   I'll mace your face unmercifully — *(Pulls mace.)*
> LEE. You'll mace my face? I'll rip off your tee —
> SHERILEE. *(Pulling knife.)* And I'll slice your dice into filigree

You treat us with such enmity —
I'll cut off your extremity — *(Lee backs off.)*
I'll shorten your longevity
And do it with great levity — *(He exits.)*
That's it, crawl away, you ugly piece
Of shit — you can — *(Shouts.)*
Hey, *kiss my ass* — you *cheapo* — *weirdo* — *kiss my* —
MERRILEE. Sherilee — Sherilee —
Everything's gotta rhyme with E.
SHERILEE. Okay then — *kiss my knee* ... you *S.O.B.*
And take your dollar twenty-three
And your teenie dick down to Avenue B
And find yourself some chimpanzee
With a crack-crazed pimp and some bad V.D.
And I hope she gives you H.I.V.
And puts your motherfuckin' ass in the cem-e-tery — eee? —
eee?
(Merrilee pulls her back to reality. She calms down — smiles — they sing sweetly)
MERILEE. Buy one — get one free
Buy me — I'll throw in —
SHERILEE. Me — It's the deal —
MERRILEE. It's the steal of the century.
BOTH. Buy one, 'n' get one free — ee — ee
Buy one, get one free —
(Lights fade.)

BLIND WILLIE AND THE TALKING DOG

BLIND WILLIE. *(Sings.)*
Have you ever been somewhere
Where the sun don't never shine
Where you never see a smile
'Cause it's midnight all the time
Only sunshine comes from the sweet red wine

Wa-wa-wa-wa-wa-wa-wa. *(Harmonica.)*
Hello — hello? Is anybody there? If anybody is there, please don't be shy — step up with a nickel or a dime. I won't be able to see it shine. But it'll help feed this old dog of mine — this mangy hungry skin-and-bones ol' dog of —
DOG. Hey, cut that shit out.
BLIND WILLIE. Quiet —
DOG. I'm not mangy — and I'm not skin-and-bones — They can see that, you know — you can't see but they can see, for Chrissake. You've got to remember, *you're* the blind one — You're the one who —
BLIND WILLIE. Quiet, they can —
DOG. Nobody's here — can you accept that? There hasn't been anybody by here for half an hour. Jesus, can't you tell if somebody's here or not? You'd think you'd have developed a *sense* by now — an acute awareness or sixth sense or something.
BLIND WILLIE.
 I woke up this morning,
 I was blue as I could be —
 I reached —
DOG. "Woke up this mornin'" — "Woke up this mornin'" —
BLIND WILLIE. Shhh. Somebody could walk up and —
DOG. And what? What? And discover that you have a talking dog? The world's one and only talking dog? Oh, that *would* be a disaster, wouldn't it — That would drive them away, wouldn't it? — That would drive them away in droves —
BLIND WILLIE.
 I need a sweet lovin' woman, rock me all night long,
 I need a sweet lovin' momma, rock me all night long.
DOG and BLIND WILLIE.
 If she loves me right, I'll never do her wrong.
DOG.
 I want a two-assed woman who'll work one of 'em off for me.
(Blind Willie stops.) Come on — lemme take one verse — come on — *(A capella:)*
 I want a two-assed woman who'll work one of 'em —
Come on — nobody's here —
BLIND WILLIE. It's not natural — a dog singing about wanting

a woman.
DOG. Natural?
BLIND WILLIE. It's *perverted.*
DOG. Perverted. I'll tell you what is really perverted — the world's one and only legitimate authentic talking dog — pretending he can't talk — pretending he is only another run-of-the-mill mongrel, pretending to be just an ordinary dog — where is the sense in that? — Where is the logic in that kind of *waste?*
BLIND WILLIE. They don't want to hear that —
DOG. What *they* don't want to hear — they don't want to hear how you woke up this mornin' just as blue as you can be — they don't want to hear it —
BLIND WILLIE. They haven't had a chance to hear it — they —
DOG. They've had a chance — they've had a million chances. They walk right by. They don't like it. Can you see that? — Ha — can you *sense* that? — Can you hear their footsteps walking by? — Not stopping?
BLIND WILLIE.
   I want a true lovin' woman —
DOG. And I want to *eat* — I want to eat in a style of the world's only talking dog. I don't want to drink muddy water and sleep in a hollow log. I don't want — what about what I want to hear? I might like to hear the quiet lap of the ocean on the beach at Waikiki — I might like to hear a hushed silence at a command performance before the crowned heads of Europe — I might like to hear the president say, "Barney, I'd like to shake your paw and tell you that the First Lady and myself — "
BLIND WILLIE. I'll throw up if I have to hear one more fucking time about the fucking president shaking your fucking paw —
DOG. *That* is exactly what would happen. The world's first and only talking dog — there would be so much money and fame and applause —
BLIND WILLIE. For who? For *you*, right? Not for us — Not for any *talent* we might have — but just because by chance you happen to be able to talk — not due to —
DOG. *Happen to be able to talk?* Do you hear yourself, for God's sake? Can you at least hear your own idiotic words coming out of your own mouth?

BLIND WILLIE. Somebody's coming —
 I'm going to Chicago, baby, I can't take you —
DOG. Nobody's coming.
BLIND WILLIE. I hear somebody —
 Goin' to Chicago, baby, I can't take you —
 Nothin' in Chicago a monkey woman —
DOG. Nobody's coming.
BLIND WILLIE. You might not tell me — you might just be deceitful enough to let them walk right up an' hear you talking —
DOG. Oh, *that* would be deceitful — that would be selfish ... An act of blind ambition — Ha — Ruthless. We would be "eating filet mignon and sleeping on a feather bed" — You can't face it — You can't accept the fact that our ticket to the big time —
BLIND WILLIE. I am supporting this team — I am the singer and the accompanist and the booker and the road manager. You are the *dog*. You hear me? I may be blind, and I may be a failure, but I am a failure — of a *man* — you are a fucking dog. D-O-G.
DOG. I am a dog because you keep me a dog. You make me a dog. I was born with a magic in me — You're hiding my magic under a bushel and we're not making it — and I'm *starving*.
BLIND WILLIE. You're not starving.
DOG. I am — I'm hungry and mangy.
BLIND WILLIE. You're *not*.
DOG. I'm a bag of bones.
BLIND WILLIE. You're not.
DOG. How would you know? — You don't even pet me anymore — You don't scratch my ears or rub my stomach — or play with me — or throw things for me to fetch —
BLIND WILLIE. Oh, God — *(Reaches into pocket — pulls out harmonica — tosses it — lets go of leash.)* Fetch —
DOG. Fuck you.
BLIND WILLIE. You can squash the spirit in a man, do you know that? — You can kill the music in a man —
DOG. And I'm not a *fucking* dog.
BLIND WILLIE. I didn't mean that — you get me so crazy sometimes —
DOG. I mean I'm not a *fucking* dog — literally. I'm not a fucking dog, because I'm not getting any fucking. *(Blind Willie sighs.)*

And I don't mean perversely, like a dog wanting a woman. I mean *normally*. Normal canine desires —
BLIND WILLIE.
   I woke up this mornin' —
DOG. I wake up cold and hungry and itching from flea bites and horny and rubbed raw from that damned leash — a leash on the world's one and only —
BLIND WILLIE. Stop!
DOG. Talking dog —
BLIND WILLIE. I've got to do it this way — to make it *this way* — You've known that — You've always known that. It's not that I've ever lied to you — This is what I *have* to do —
DOG. What about what I have to do? What about the gift that I was born with? What about hiding my light under a bushel so that —
BLIND WILLIE. What do you want? You want to be free? Is that what you want?
DOG. I only want to —
BLIND WILLIE. You want to do a single? I'm holding you back? — You want to go out on your own? Go ahead — let them marvel at the voice — The world's one and only talking dog — I also thought you were the world's only talking dog *friend* — Ha — Oh, they'll marvel at the voice — the wonderful voice — waa — but they're not just gonna *listen* to that voice — they're not just gonna buy the records and stand in line to hear it at Caesar's Palace — They're gonna wanna know where that voice is *coming* from — those scientists — those *vivisectionists* — They're gonna have to know, *why* is that voice coming out of a dog — They're gonna have to tear open that little throat and rip out those unique little vocal chords and put them under a microscope — and —
DOG. Willie —
BLIND WILLIE. Go — I'm misusing you — I'm degrading you — go! Give my regards to the president — shake his paw for me.
DOG. He'll shake *my* paw.
BLIND WILLIE. He can shake your dick for all I care — He can put you away with the First Lady — go — I'm sick of being a trampler of talent. I'm sick of standing between you and Acapulco — and filet mignon —
DOG. Willie? — Willie — we can go *together*.

BLIND WILLIE. As what? — As Barney the Fabulous Talking Dog and his Blind Boy on a Leash? — Oh, isn't he loyal? — He had that blind man when he first got started and now that he's a star, he still keeps him around — That's a man for you — they're loyal — that man's seventy-three now — that's twelve dog years — twelve years old and blind but still loyal — they say the blind man sleeps at the foot of his bed.
DOG. Willie.
BLIND WILLIE. And barks in case of fire — and *sings* in case of fire —
    Wake up, wake up,
    Talkin' Dog
    Your house is burnin' down
    Wake up Mister Superstar
    Your house is burnin' down
    Wake up yo' birch and them ugly fuckin' puppies —
(He starts to cry.)
DOG. Willie — Willie — somebody's coming —
BLIND WILLIE. You talk to them — get discovered —
DOG. Come on —
BLIND WILLIE. I can't help it if I've got to do it my way.
DOG. I know that.
BLIND WILLIE. I just couldn't be the old man at the end of the leash.
DOG. You've always been honest.
BLIND WILLIE. I just couldn't handle it — some people can handle it — I can't.
DOG. I've always know that — You've always been straight ahead — People do love blues, you know — If they'd just stop and listen — Well ... see you, Willie —
BLIND WILLIE. Yeah — See ya ...
    I once had a friend, Barney was his name —
DOG. Oh, God.
BLIND WILLIE.
    I once had a friend and Barney was his name.
DOG. I'm goin', Willie — I am — *(He exits.)*
BLIND WILLIE.
    But he left me in the darkness chasin' after money and fame.

I once found a puppy at the A.S.P.C.A.
Found a little homeless puppy at the A.S.P.C.A.
He was wet and sick and skinny
But I loved him anyway.
Took him home in a snowstorm
Lord, he was almost dead
Wrapped him up in my only blanket
Gave him some milk and bread
And when he got distemper
I held his little pukey head.
Spent every cent I'd been savin'
To get him his license and his shots
Used my white can for firewood
To keep the room nice and hot
But he left me blind, alone and helpless
That's the thanks I got
If I hadn't come along
They would of gassed him for sure
If I hadn't bought him that milkbone
I wouldn't be so destitute and poor
But he wants to do a single
Oh Lord, where can I ...

(Dog sits next to him.)

I'm Blind Willie Johnson
Me and my old dog Jim?

DOG. Jim? Jim?
BLIND WILLIE.

The president shook his paw — my good ol' dog Jim
He's a true blue friend
And I can really count on him.

End of Evening

PROPERTY LIST

Lump covered with blanket
Bed
Laundry scale, ladder, blue laundry bag with blouse
Table and chairs
Witness stand
Electric chair
Purse with oatmeal bowl, shopping bag (SYLVIA)
Beer can, pointed "Bus Stop" sign (IRWIN)
Whistle (DAD)
Chair (BENDER)
"Smile" sign (JIMBO)
Switchblades (JIMBO, GIBBY)
Laundry bag, purse with ticket and money (MARIANNE)
Newspaper, pencil and pad (GEORGE)
Letter (GEORGE)
Vial of white powder, Polaroids (GEORGE)
Laundry bag (KENNETH)
Straw hats (LUCY, PETE)
Pencil and pad, plate and fork (PETE)
Pot with meat and potatoes and spoon (LUCY)
Cloth, piece of meat (INSPECTOR)
Pencil and pad, brains (SERGEANT)
Plant and pot with meat underneath, hat with two potatoes
    (INSPECTOR)
Meat, pot (PROSECUTOR)
Bible (CLERGYMAN)
Three foil-wrapped potatoes (EXECUTIONER)
"Buy one, get one free" sign (MERRILEE, SHERILEE)
Mace (MERRILEE)
Knife (SHERILEE)
Harmonica (BLIND WILLIE)

SOUND EFFECTS

Swelling romantic music

NEW PLAYS

★ **YELLOW FACE by David Henry Hwang.** Asian-American playwright DHH leads a protest against the casting of Jonathan Pryce as the Eurasian pimp in the original Broadway production of *Miss Saigon*, condemning the practice as "yellowface." The lines between truth and fiction blur with hilarious and moving results in this unreliable memoir. "A pungent play of ideas with a big heart." –*Variety.* "Fabulously inventive." –*The New Yorker.* [5M, 2W] ISBN: 978-0-8222-2301-6

★ **33 VARIATIONS by Moisés Kaufmann.** A mother coming to terms with her daughter. A composer coming to terms with his genius. And, even though they're separated by 200 years, these two people share an obsession that might, even just for a moment, make time stand still. "A compellingly original and thoroughly watchable play for today." –*Talkin' Broadway.* [4M, 4W] ISBN: 978-0-8222-2392-4

★ **BOOM by Peter Sinn Nachtrieb.** A grad student's online personal ad lures a mysterious journalism student to his subterranean research lab. But when a major catastrophic event strikes the planet, their date takes on evolutionary significance and the fate of humanity hangs in the balance. "Darkly funny dialogue." –*NY Times.* "Literate, coarse, thoughtful, sweet, scabrously inappropriate." –*Washington City Paper.* [1M, 2W] ISBN: 978-0-8222-2370-2

★ **LOVE, LOSS AND WHAT I WORE by Nora Ephron and Delia Ephron, based on the book by Ilene Beckerman.** A play of monologues and ensemble pieces about women, clothes and memory covering all the important subjects—mothers, prom dresses, mothers, buying bras, mothers, hating purses and why we only wear black. "Funny, compelling." –*NY Times.* "So funny and so powerful." –*WowOwow.com.* [5W] ISBN: 978-0-8222-2355-9

★ **CIRCLE MIRROR TRANSFORMATION by Annie Baker.** When four lost New Englanders enrolled in Marty's community center drama class experiment with harmless games, hearts are quietly torn apart, and tiny wars of epic proportions are waged and won. "Absorbing, unblinking and sharply funny." –*NY Times.* [2M, 3W] ISBN: 978-0-8222-2445-7

★ **BROKE-OLOGY by Nathan Louis Jackson.** The King family has weathered the hardships of life and survived with their love for each other intact. But when two brothers are called home to take care of their father, they find themselves strangely at odds. "Engaging dialogue." –*TheaterMania.com.* "Assured, bighearted." –*Time Out.* [3M, 1W] ISBN: 978-0-8222-2428-0

DRAMATISTS PLAY SERVICE, INC.
440 Park Avenue South, New York, NY 10016   212-683-8960   Fax 212-213-1539
postmaster@dramatists.com   www.dramatists.com

NEW PLAYS

★ **A CIVIL WAR CHRISTMAS: AN AMERICAN MUSICAL CELEBRATION by Paula Vogel, music by Daryl Waters.** It's 1864, and Washington, D.C. is settling down to the coldest Christmas Eve in years. Intertwining many lives, this musical shows us that the gladness of one's heart is the best gift of all. "Boldly inventive theater, warm and affecting." –*Talkin' Broadway.* "Crisp strokes of dialogue." –*NY Times.* [12M, 5W] ISBN: 978-0-8222-2361-0

★ **SPEECH & DEBATE by Stephen Karam.** Three teenage misfits in Salem, Oregon discover they are linked by a sex scandal that's rocked their town. "Savvy comedy." –*Variety.* "Hilarious, cliché-free, and immensely entertaining." –*NY Times.* "A strong, rangy play." –*NY Newsday.* [2M, 2W] ISBN: 978-0-8222-2286-6

★ **DIVIDING THE ESTATE by Horton Foote.** Matriarch Stella Gordon is determined not to divide her 100-year-old Texas estate, despite her family's declining wealth and the looming financial crisis. But her three children have another plan. "Goes for laughs and succeeds." –*NY Daily News.* "The theatrical equivalent of a page-turner." –*Bloomberg.com.* [4M, 9W] ISBN: 978-0-8222-2398-6

★ **WHY TORTURE IS WRONG, AND THE PEOPLE WHO LOVE THEM by Christopher Durang.** Christopher Durang turns political humor upside down with this raucous and provocative satire about America's growing homeland "insecurity." "A smashing new play." –*NY Observer.* "You may laugh yourself silly." –*Bloomberg News.* [4M, 3W] ISBN: 978-0-8222-2401-3

★ **FIFTY WORDS by Michael Weller.** While their nine-year-old son is away for the night on his first sleepover, Adam and Jan have an evening alone together, beginning a suspenseful nightlong roller-coaster ride of revelation, rancor, passion and humor. "Mr. Weller is a bold and productive dramatist." –*NY Times.* [1M, 1W] ISBN: 978-0-8222-2348-1

★ **BECKY'S NEW CAR by Steven Dietz.** Becky Foster is caught in middle age, middle management and in a middling marriage—with no prospects for change on the horizon. Then one night a socially inept and grief-struck millionaire stumbles into the car dealership where Becky works. "Gently and consistently funny." –*Variety.* "Perfect blend of hilarious comedy and substantial weight." –*Broadway Hour.* [4M, 3W] ISBN: 978-0-8222-2393-1

DRAMATISTS PLAY SERVICE, INC.
440 Park Avenue South, New York, NY 10016   212-683-8960   Fax 212-213-1539
postmaster@dramatists.com   www.dramatists.com

NEW PLAYS

★ **AT HOME AT THE ZOO by Edward Albee.** Edward Albee delves deeper into his play THE ZOO STORY by adding a first act, HOMELIFE, which precedes Peter's fateful meeting with Jerry on a park bench in Central Park. "An essential and heartening experience." *–NY Times.* "Darkly comic and thrilling." *–Time Out.* "Genuinely fascinating." *–Journal News.* [2M, 1W] ISBN: 978-0-8222-2317-7

★ **PASSING STRANGE book and lyrics by Stew, music by Stew and Heidi Rodewald, created in collaboration with Annie Dorsen.** A daring musical about a young bohemian that takes you from black middle-class America to Amsterdam, Berlin and beyond on a journey towards personal and artistic authenticity. "Fresh, exuberant, bracingly inventive, bitingly funny, and full of heart." *–NY Times.* "The freshest musical in town!" *–Wall Street Journal.* "Excellent songs and a vulnerable heart." *–Variety.* [4M, 3W] ISBN: 978-0-8222-2400-6

★ **REASONS TO BE PRETTY by Neil LaBute.** Greg really, truly adores his girlfriend, Steph. Unfortunately, he also thinks she has a few physical imperfections, and when he mentions them, all hell breaks loose. "Tight, tense and emotionally true." *–Time Magazine.* "Lively and compulsively watchable." *–The Record.* [2M, 2W] ISBN: 978-0-8222-2394-8

★ **OPUS by Michael Hollinger.** With only a few days to rehearse a grueling Beethoven masterpiece, a world-class string quartet struggles to prepare their highest-profile performance ever—a televised ceremony at the White House. "Intimate, intense and profoundly moving." *–Time Out.* "Worthy of scores of bravissimos." *–BroadwayWorld.com.* [4M, 1W] ISBN: 978-0-8222-2363-4

★ **BECKY SHAW by Gina Gionfriddo.** When an evening calculated to bring happiness takes a dark turn, crisis and comedy ensue in this wickedly funny play that asks what we owe the people we love and the strangers who land on our doorstep. "As engrossing as it is ferociously funny." *–NY Times.* "Gionfriddo is some kind of genius." *–Variety.* [2M, 3W] ISBN: 978-0-8222-2402-0

★ **KICKING A DEAD HORSE by Sam Shepard.** Hobart Struther's horse has just dropped dead. In an eighty-minute monologue, he discusses what path brought him here in the first place, the fate of his marriage, his career, politics and eventually the nature of the universe. "Deeply instinctual and intuitive." *–NY Times.* "The brilliance is in the infinite reverberations Shepard extracts from his simple metaphor." *–TheaterMania.* [1M, 1W] ISBN: 978-0-8222-2336-8

DRAMATISTS PLAY SERVICE, INC.
440 Park Avenue South, New York, NY 10016   212-683-8960   Fax 212-213-1539
postmaster@dramatists.com   www.dramatists.com

NEW PLAYS

★ **AUGUST: OSAGE COUNTY by Tracy Letts.** WINNER OF THE 2008 PULITZER PRIZE AND TONY AWARD. When the large Weston family reunites after Dad disappears, their Oklahoma homestead explodes in a maelstrom of repressed truths and unsettling secrets. "Fiercely funny and bitingly sad." –*NY Times*. "Ferociously entertaining." –*Variety*. "A hugely ambitious, highly combustible saga." –*NY Daily News*. [6M, 7W] ISBN: 978-0-8222-2300-9

★ **RUINED by Lynn Nottage.** WINNER OF THE 2009 PULITZER PRIZE. Set in a small mining town in Democratic Republic of Congo, RUINED is a haunting, probing work about the resilience of the human spirit during times of war. "A full-immersion drama of shocking complexity and moral ambiguity." –*Variety*. "Sincere, passionate, courageous." –*Chicago Tribune*. [8M, 4W] ISBN: 978-0-8222-2390-0

★ **GOD OF CARNAGE by Yasmina Reza, translated by Christopher Hampton.** WINNER OF THE 2009 TONY AWARD. A playground altercation between boys brings together their Brooklyn parents, leaving the couples in tatters as the rum flows and tensions explode. "Satisfyingly primitive entertainment." –*NY Times*. "Elegant, acerbic, entertainingly fueled on pure bile." –*Variety*. [2M, 2W] ISBN: 978-0-8222-2399-3

★ **THE SEAFARER by Conor McPherson.** Sharky has returned to Dublin to look after his irascible, aging brother. Old drinking buddies Ivan and Nicky are holed up at the house too, hoping to play some cards. But with the arrival of a stranger from the distant past, the stakes are raised ever higher. "Dark and enthralling Christmas fable." –*NY Times*. "A timeless classic." –*Hollywood Reporter*. [5M] ISBN: 978-0-8222-2284-2

★ **THE NEW CENTURY by Paul Rudnick.** When the playwright is Paul Rudnick, expectations are geared for a play both hilarious and smart, and this provocative and outrageous comedy is no exception. "The one-liners fly like rockets." –*NY Times*. "The funniest playwright around." –*Journal News*. [2M, 3W] ISBN: 978-0-8222-2315-3

★ **SHIPWRECKED! AN ENTERTAINMENT—THE AMAZING ADVENTURES OF LOUIS DE ROUGEMONT (AS TOLD BY HIMSELF) by Donald Margulies.** The amazing story of bravery, survival and celebrity that left nineteenth-century England spellbound. Dare to be whisked away. "A deft, literate narrative." –*LA Times*. "Springs to life like a theatrical pop-up book." –*NY Times*. [2M, 1W] ISBN: 978-0-8222-2341-2

DRAMATISTS PLAY SERVICE, INC.
440 Park Avenue South, New York, NY 10016   212-683-8960   Fax 212-213-1539
postmaster@dramatists.com   www.dramatists.com